GPS

God Positioning Spirit

Personal Navigator
from Despair to Destiny

DEANNA BROWN

GPS: God Positioning Spirit

ISBN-13: 978-1-938886-64-5
ISBN-10: 193888664X

Printed in the United States of America
First Printing: 2013

Dedication

I dedicate this book to the participants who contributed to my emotional and spiritual growth, especially to the precious souls whose lives I made difficult along the way: I ask your forgiveness. Sometimes it's difficult to comprehend we're created in Gods image from pure love intended to cultivate our gift to share added value to others while we journey together.

Special heartfelt thanks to:

Rick, My God Appointed Husband, the love and joy of my life, for his compassion, commitment and consistent support and help proof reading the manuscript, and for his contribution to this book and most importantly for his prayers.

To our children I thank you, for your suggestion for me to write my life experience through the process of discovery. How God's Positioning Spirit my personal navigator, repositioned my life from despair to destiny.

Our Children

Especially to Danny, Sandi, Paul, Frank, Hope, Karyn, and Jojo, I can only imagine what you endured as children. You were subjected to abandonment, uncertainty and chaos early in your lives, and transformed those unbearable experiences into character-building life lessons and breaking the code of dysfunction. We built a value based family foundation of resilience, love, trust and faith for our future generations. I also thank God for Megan who openly accepted us with unconditional love as family.

Acknowledgements

"But the Helper, the Holy Spirit, whom the Father will send in my name, he will teach you all things and bring to your remembrance all that I have said to you." **John 14:26**

I would like to acknowledge the Anthony Robbins Foundation, a non-profit organization created to make a significant difference in the quality of life for people who are often forgotten, youth, the homeless and hungry, prisoners, the elderly, and the disabled. Change takes place when a person gives of them self to improve the quality of life for another.

Foundation staff and countless volunteers, your heartfelt commitment is truly a gift.

Tony Robbins, for paving the way and teaching millions we are the voice for God.

And especially to Michelle Podlensi for all of the coaching, mentoring and hand holding she provided during the entire process of writing this book. I could not have completed this book without her help.

Mentors: Bob Baker, Kathy Camarillo, Trudy London, Joy Karanick, Cheryl Jackson, Dusty Kemp, Michelle Newhouse, Alicia Mendeke, Michelle Podlensi, Arvee Robinson, Tony Robbins, Jim Schmidt, Kathleen Sharp and Joe Faulger (for your encouragement to voice my story).

Special thanks for your support and Contribution with Self Mastery Youth Leadership Program: Joe Coto, Lorraine Guerin, Tim McDonough, Terry Maxie, Cindy Dwyer, Beverly Hart, Eileen Patron, J. Manuel Herrera, Susan and Lee Clark, the late Nadine Potter, Sam Jones, Paul

Lerma, John and Jo Lopez (upstairs records Inc.) and the Anthony Robbins Foundation Scholarship and Mentoring Program.

Self-Mastery Alumni Advisory Board: Alondra Alvarez, Fatima Amuezcua, Lydia Desimone, Maggie Castellon, Andreas Lara, Nohemi Reyes, Tina Sanchez, Sylvia Ornales Wise, and Yvette Valenzuela for your commitment with over 15 years of volunteer service.

Guardian Angels in work clothes: Thank you!

Chris Ramos, who unknowingly shared his 2003 accident story, which gave comforting assurance that Sandi, my daughter, would recover from a coma caused by a car accident.

I wish to thank Emo Loredo for your commitment during the primary stages writing the manuscript. Your enduring patience, sense of humor, instructional writing assistance and editing was inspirational.

I also wish to thank Chewah Slater and Kaine Thompson for your editing services. And to Len Futaba for emergency technical support and Lou Podlesni for expert webpage services.

And to my granddaughter, Taylor Garcia, who spent tireless hours meticulously reading and processing questions that helped format structure to the Process of Discovery workbook.

And, of course, Ann McIndoo, my Author's Coach, who is amazing; her guidance tools and strategies work!

Contents

Process of Discovery through Rebirth

Displaced

Direction

Destiny

Foreword

For years, I had shied away from traditional life coaches. I felt that I did not need motivation with the level of ambition I already had, or the coaches I had met did not walk the talk and had nothing to teach me. The bottom line was I did not connect with many folks and felt they could not add value to my life.

I already had everything. I was 34, had a beautiful wife and three amazing daughters, and a career in Financial Services that provided many choices and luxuries for my family. Based in Hong Kong, I had worked in Singapore, Sydney and London. I travelled extensively and could do pretty much anything I wanted. I had everything in my life that I had always wanted as a boy, and more.

Yet, I did not feel truly fulfilled. I once heard someone say that a life of abundance with no fulfillment is the ultimate failure. They were right. Something was missing in my life, and I had no idea what it was. For me to feel like this made me angry. I had fantastic people in my life that cared and loved me. To believe that something was missing made me feel guilty.

After I met Deanna in 2012, I realized that I had misjudged the value of a coach. I found that I needed someone who could guide me beyond the superficial state I had lived in for so long; a coach who could help me steer through the new emotions I found as a result of an awakening experience . . . I saw God for the first time in my life.

I was at a conference. I was relaxed and in a semi-conscious state, when I "saw" an old man, a black man, staring at me. He was in a lot of pain. Several minutes in to this vision, he looked away from me. He looked to his right hand side. I felt immense physical pain and sadness. My heart ached. I had neck pain. I was nearly yelling out for him to look back at me. I will never forget this feeling of total abandonment. Several minutes later, he looked back at me. My heart filled with physical warmth, right in the center of my chest. I felt heat in my hands. It was a moment of pure love. I then went into a deep state of relaxation.

My belief is that this vision, this gift, was to teach me that God has always been in me, through all the years that my parents taught me about him. I needed to let Him in and have faith. I had looked away from Him for so long, just like He did to me in this experience.

Later the next day, I met Deanna. She walked by me, and I stopped her. She looked right at me. There were no words. I stared into Deanna's eyes and she knew that I had seen God. She knew I had found my path. We didn't say much to one another, other than exchange details and promise to be in touch.

I have spoken to Deanna every week since. I have experienced unimaginable changes in my life. I returned home to my wonderful family. Deanna has been enormously helpful in aligning my personal life changes to the lives of those whom I love the most.

My wife, too, has started to speak to Deanna regularly. In four days, I increased the funding for my business. I opened offices in Hong Kong and London within four months. I signed up every client I wanted and hired 15 people.

The relationship I have with Deanna has given me a guide through these newfound feelings of faith, freedom and clarity. She has taught me how to stay focused on my values at a phase of enormous release and growth.

How do I feel today? There is only one word: Guided. Totally! There is a certainty that I am on a path to my destiny. I do not know where it is going, but I know there is a plan and that I am moving in the right direction. The reason for this is my belief in something far greater.

After 34 years, I have started a relationship with God. Not a relationship yet of worship, just an awareness of our Maker, and the trust and belief that He is always with us.

To find this path, to allow God to position us as He has planned . . . this is when your life begins and your real potential, a level that was before unimaginable, starts to materialize.

With so much going on with my newfound direction and fearless approach to life, "staying in the present" has become a real goal. This is something that Deanna talks about at length.

Like many coaching relationships, it is a journey. I feel privileged to have met Deanna as I made the right turn down the highway of my life. She is certainly someone who I would like to stay with on this journey for many years ahead.

As you read this book, you will experience Deanna's journey and I hope that through her life and the revelations she has received, you will find God, receive GPS, and start walking your own path of destiny.

Sam Jones
Founder and CEO, CompIndex Corporation

Introduction

Have you ever wondered about the meaning of life? Especially during a terrible experience that has left you feeling overwhelmed and hopeless, as though you were on a dead-end road without direction or a GPS?

Before I was born, if God had given me a sneak preview of even half my life trials, I would have pleaded mercy and asked not to be born.

As it turned out, my parents were the obvious match from which I needed to learn what not to do, which innately helped prepare me for my life and my destiny. Nonetheless, many of my parent's unhealthy traits filtered deep into my psyche. I duplicated much of their self-destructive behavior throughout my early adult years: rejected by my mom at age 14, married at 15, and mother to seven kids by the time I was 23. Under the guise of love, I endured one abusive relationship after another, believing that physical abuse was the demonstration of love and part of life.

Unable to find my way out of an abyss of darkness created by years of emotional despair, my mind short-circuited. I was institutionalized at Agnews State Mental Hospital. Having no support system to guide me, I was like a magnet attracting people who were loaded on drugs or drunk like me, recycling the same old stories, only adding a little more drama than the previous one. The very thing I despised about my family when I was young became my template for life, running the blame game in my mind about how unjust people and life were, all the while being part of the dysfunction. I lived a double-standard life, working in the nursing profession and trying to be a functioning mom while at the same time, self-destructive, without hope, heading towards a disastrous collision. I was haunted by my past, unable to turn my life around. Eventually, one by one, my teenaged kids moved away to find sanity within their own lives.

One night, alone, physically drained, mentally exhausted, and without direction and in desperation, I hit bottom. When suddenly from my core I became explosive, like a raving lunatic, angry with God, I spouted everything, shouting directives, and screaming "I was a mistake. Why God! Why did you create me?" I questioned God's intention, sobbing hysterically, hoping that God would hear me in heaven, while ranting my hostility toward Him.

Then, suddenly to my surprise, God made a house call. His Spirit embraced me with *"Pure Love"* that transformed every fiber of my being. I was healed from addiction; pain-filled memories no longer bound me but became reminders to move forward, and revealed that life has meaning. To my surprise, God's Positioning Spirit (GPS) was always within my reach, ready to mentor me throughout my life. *"We're Never Alone"*

This book is about how the Creator of the Universe became my personal GPS to navigate life's obstacle course. When I was much younger, I heard that God created everything on earth and lived in heaven. It was mindboggling to me. How could God know and help me, one person in the midst of a billion souls on earth. To me, life was bleak and offered one certainty—I was alone, left to my own devices to figure it all out through trial, error, pain, and frustration.

As humans, our nature is to desire and seek comfort and security, but this runs counter to our best interest and spiritual growth. We are made to be resilient, not rigid. Yet, many people choose the easy way out because, as Alice Walker said, "The most common way people give up their power is by thinking they don't have any." They begin to feel powerless, blinded by fear, and stay where they are no matter how bad it is and no matter how deep the pain.

There is a better way.

I have learned that pain signifies the need to push through the illusion and make a breakthrough. I discovered life is a Process of Discovery:

Position: The first critical step was to Position my life to move forward. I needed to learn to love, to believe in myself, and to identify what was causing me pain and to take a different approach to becoming accountable as a participant in my own life.

Promise: I realized that even though I loved my parents, their life choices were not the route I wanted to travel for my children or myself. This revelation required me to find mentors whose values reflected the life I imagined myself living; awakening a Promise long-desired to be fulfilled.

Passion: I knew no one was going to come to my rescue. If anyone did, I realized, there would be a tradeoff, a condition attached. Therefore, I needed to learn the meaning of love and apply it to myself. I needed to change all of the destructive associations linked to my past and develop a mind-set of possibilities fueled with Passion to move me forward.

Purpose: Finally, the most healing step was forgiveness. When I forgave myself, my parents, and everyone else who had caused me pain, I began to heal. It was amazing to realize that the most painful, challenging, and humbling experiences of my life were essential components necessary for me to fulfill my life's Purpose.

The truth is that we are all essential, hand-picked by our Creator to fulfill our destiny. I believe each soul has purpose on earth intended to make a difference in people's lives, which requires us to "become" the difference first. Therefore, by learning to trust in our potential through our life trials, which helps to define our character as we walk our talk, then we can teach by our example and will be able to touch lives.

If you are on a quest to find meaning in your life but disheartening experiences have inhibited you from moving forward, I suggest you view the situation from a different perspective. You know intuitively what you desire in life. Perception, focus, and meaning are everything. Ask yourself: *What must I do differently to redirect my life? How will it add value to my loved ones, others, and me? What must I stop thinking about that keeps me stuck in the pain? What will the changes mean to me? How committed am I to set-up new standards to live by?*

We are not mistakes. Our life challenges have a purpose. They define our commitment through our process of discovery, or our personalized journey of learning how to defy the odds. Life offers many opportunities to break through the barriers of resistance. A bodybuilder lifting weights experiences the pain of burning muscles, but it's the burn that drives him to raise the bar of resistance, to push toward specific objectives. Similarly, our primary objective must be to build character and to reposition our pain for purpose rather than allowing it to defeat us.

Emotional hardships and uncertain times—economic recessions, for example—provide opportunities for us to reassess our priorities, especially when life comes to a standstill. What is so amazing is that it is at this point that our innate, creative gifts come to the surface. Sometimes by admitting to yourself that you are unable to do it alone and ask God for guidance, you allow the reservoir of God's resources to flow through you to create lasting change for yourself and a greater good for humanity.

The Mayans got it right. Their 2012 predictions, despite the misinterpretations that they foreshadowed the end of the world, were not far from the truth. Perhaps their message was intended to signify a planet broken by the end of an era, to begin an era of spiritual awakening. Or perhaps, it was a revelation reminder of what we have been entrusted. If Earth reflects man's state-of-mind, then we must first take courage to face ourselves. Only then will we give the Earth and ourselves permission to flourish.

Within all human beings resides a solution; it is etched upon our souls. Imagine a combination of awakened perspectives, unique attributes and gifts, and life's lessons from the "school of hard knocks," becoming the vehicle by which we create a global solution! It is mind boggling to comprehend how our pain positions us for purpose and becomes the catalyst that gives value to our lives. Nothing goes to waste, even in the most devastating experiences.

Ask yourself: *If I were God what would I do differently? Would I create a perfect world if such an act were possible? What would be the outcome?* In theory, you could create such a world, but if you did there would be no problems to learn from, no changes to be made, no purpose to fulfill. Life is like a scale. It requires polar opposites to balance it. The point I wish to make is that there is no experience, no aspect, and no facet of life that God can't use to create a value that surpasses the comfort of normalcy or numbness.

In GPS (God Positioning Spirit), I use my story as an example of how we can move from struggle to success. I do this not to draw attention to my story, but to show how divine intervention can chisel through a hardened heart and use a painful past to change a life script. In my case, God helped me see that dreams really can come true.

He used my trials to prepare me for my profession as an international life coach. Positioning me to help a wide variety of people—from entrepreneurs to executives, from "at risk" youths to emotional and physical imprisoned souls, who desire to create change within themselves and their circumstances.

On a personal level, I never would have imagined having a beautiful waterfront wedding in Santa Barbara, California, with my kids and grandchildren in the wedding party; or getting to travel extensively, staying at five star hotels, golfing, sailing, having fun in the process of embracing every moment with gratitude with Rick, my husband of 24 years and the love of my life.

And most importantly, I would never have believed that my family, our children who are now adults with families of their own, would continue to pass on the key fabric of life—love, connection and respect for each other, viewing life from God's perspective which helps us to stay focused, building a legacy for future generations.

We are linked by threads that weave us together into a magnificent, priceless tapestry.

"Be the CHANGE you wish to see in THE WORLD" - **Gandhi**

Preface

Not long ago I was invited to attend a seminar by motivational speaker, Brendon Burchard. There was a mixed crowd of enthusiastic people waiting to enter the event, many of whom were engaged in diverse conversations, and many who appeared quiet and kept to themselves. I was standing near a couple and started talking to them. I asked what they expected to learn from the event, and they said, "Tools to redirect our lives." They asked what I did for a living and I mentioned I was writing a book. I began to share my views on "repositioning pain for purpose" as a concept. The couple indicated more interest in moving away from the pain by learning skills to help them move on with their lives.

I learned that the husband was diagnosed with rheumatoid arthritis, crippling his auto mechanic business. They almost lost everything and could not see the positive outcome from their painful experience. I informed them that pain helps us make better decisions. They weren't able to make the connection at first, so I asked what else changed in their family. The wife brought up their 15-year-old autistic son and how he required full medical attention. She mentioned how her son would watch his father take motors apart and fix them, and eventually the son started taking motors apart and putting them back together under his dad's supervision. To their astonishment, their son was able to repair motors meticulously. He required less medical attention because of his proclivity to fix cars and was able to help the family's auto mechanic business grow.

A woman in her mid-30s was listening to our conversation and began sharing her story. When she was a teenager, she was a shy, quiet girl who was raped. It crippled her emotionally and required years of psychotherapy. The real transforming factor was when she started speaking to young girls about the process of recovery from shame, which was her message. By adding value to these young girls' lives, she was healed and restored. Her confidence was off the charts and she became a high-demand public speaker. It was amazing to hear testimonies of how in their brokenness God restored and repositioned these people's lives for purpose.

My spiritual daughter, Stacy, is another example of how a painful experience positions people to seek solutions, which inspires their desire and purpose. She and her husband of ten years, Ron, wanted deeply to have a child. One night while dining at a restaurant, she became ill and was rushed to the hospital. While there, she discovered she was four months pregnant. It was a joyous time for everyone, with friends and relatives thanking God for the miracle and a neighbor donating nursery items to her. The due date arrived and Frank was ready to receive little Jaxson in his arms. However, Jaxson was stillborn. He went from his dad's arms to the hands of God.

Long after that devastating day, Stacy became a hospital volunteer, which inspired her to complete nursing school, a plan which she had set aside years prior. After passing her exams, she became a licensed vocational nurse. She developed a business as a home care provider, specializing in preeclampsia, the condition she had during her pregnancy. She is now helping other women because she was able to reposition and repurpose her life. Every soul has a purpose. It's not the duration of a life that gives purpose—even a baby's short-lived life impacts many souls, leaving an infinite imprint on our hearts.

> *"We're predestined souls with a purpose to impact lives...Jaxson's legacy continues"*

My granddaughters, Victoria and Chandrea, who were four and three at the time, suffered a great loss when their father died, leaving their mother emotionally distraught and severely depressed. Their mother, who was my own daughter, turned to drugs, rendering her incapable of caring for the girls. My husband and I raised them for a short time; eventually Karyn become drug free and resumed full time care of her daughters. Victoria and Chandrea grew up insepa-rable. By that point, Victoria developed a strong sense of indepen-dence and responsibility, becoming a role model for her sister.

While in high school, Victoria met Manuel, a boy who had come from a similar background as Victoria's, and they instantly bonded. Their friendship turned into love. After graduating from school and se-curing jobs, Victoria and Manuel married and began planning their future. Victoria planned every detail of her wedding and was always looking for ways to improve her lifestyle with Manuel. She liked the finer things in life and was not reluctant to work for them. She worked full time yet always found time to take her grandfather, Ed, to his doctor visits after his knee surgeries. As a result, his doctors came to know her pretty well.

One rainy day at work, Victoria stepped into an employee transport van, slipped, and landed on her back, hitting the steps. In excruciat-ing pain, she was sent home to recover. Within days, she was unable to feel anything from her chest down. Fearing the worse, Manuel called 911. After waiting in the emergency room for several hours, her grandfather's doctor just happened to walk by and recognized her. He made immediate inquiries. The emergency room doctors informed him that Victoria had a broken back and spinal fluid was leaking into her body, causing her paralysis. Without hesitation, her grandfather's doctor called his neighbor, who just happened to be a world-renowned orthopedic spine surgeon, and scheduled an ap-pointment for the next day.

A CAT scan confirmed that Victoria's spinal fluid was leaking and her spine was fractured in four areas. Surgery was scheduled, but the prognosis was grim. She had a 95% chance of never walking again. An eight-hour surgery by a skilled surgeon and God's guiding hand resulted in a successful outcome. They put a titanium rod into her spine, and Victoria went through grueling residential physical thera-py. Gradually she regained her ability to walk. However, Victoria and Manuel's dream of having a family was now doubtful, even though they were only in their mid-twenties.

A few years later while driving at night through a rough neighborhood, Victoria and her sister, Chandrea, noticed three little girls playing outside in front of a cheap motel room. They felt compelled to knock on the motel room door to inquire about the children. Abruptly, the girl's mother opened the door. She appeared surprised to see the girls still playing outside. Victoria and Chandrea were also surprised, for the mother turned out to be Angie, a woman they had met years prior. Being bold, Victoria demanded to know why the girls were outside in the dark. Angie was obviously annoyed. After a few heated words exchanged regarding the girls, she abruptly told Victoria to take the girls home with her. The following morning, Chandrea and Victoria returned with the girls and were stunned when Angie requested that they keep them.

They all proceeded to a local notary office, which became the first step to adoption proceedings. Within the court system, Victoria, Chandrea, and both their husbands, spent many years battling for the girls' legal custody. Eventually they were awarded legal guardianship. Victoria's determined mindset and compassionate, humble heart were essential elements needed to provide a secure and loving home to those severely emotionally and physically abused little girls. Chandrea found completion by giving unconditional love to the youngest of the three. Both sisters got the family they dreamed of and are now raising healthy, emotionally stable children in a Christian home. All these are examples that show in each of our lives challenges have the ability to be transformed for good.

"If we live in the past it limits our future"

God Positioning Spirit
Process of Discovery

Repression

Chapter One: Despair

Search for Understanding

In my early years, I spent more time with my grandparents, along with my older brother and sister, Robert and Silvia, while my mom and dad lived in the city, trying to make their combustible marriage work. My grandparents lived in a neighborhood known as *"Salsi Puedes"* ("Get Out If You Can"), a rural area in San Jose, California, which was home to a number of famous people, including United Farm Workers pioneer César Estrada Chávez and soul singer Clifford Coulter.

My grandfather entered this country with his new 15-year-old bride as a railroad worker, laying tracks. Her mother had insisted they get married before venturing into the new land of opportunity. They never returned to Mexico.

Eventually both became migrant farm workers, working together side-by-side in the grueling California summer heat. Grandma "Nana" held her own while working in the fields. Like the other women, she covered herself up from top to bottom. Nana wore a flannel shirt and pants with a rope around her waist and covered her head with a bandana and brim hat. During off-season, she often wore a long skirt with a white blouse, blue sweater, and knee-high nylons that by the end of the day had rolled down and looked like doughnuts around her ankles. Nana was not a tall woman, but she drew attention with her shrewd smile and "eye of the tiger" eye contact. She had prominent cheekbones and dark, weathered skin. She wore her hair tightly rolled up in a bun. Her persona, combined with the Aztec Indian blood running through her veins, was well-suited for Poncho Villa's Mexican Military Revolutionary band of women.

She had a strong personality, and the people who knew her loved her. Those who experienced her wrath stood their distance, especially when she drank—including my grandpa, who for as long as I can remember lived outside in a garage detached from the main house.

Come twilight, like clockwork, she would seat herself in her favorite rocking chair on the front porch, resting her elbows on her knees, with a Prince Charles tobacco cigarette she had rolled herself hanging off the side of her lip, occasionally spitting into an empty Folgers coffee can. She sat for hours, like an eagle, perched, protecting her domain. Everyone knew her, especially the neighborhood kids. We knew she had bubble gum and candy tucked into her long skirt, which she pulled up to her knees, creating a pocket for her hankie and treats for us kids.

My grandfather, Papa, was tall and slender, with a light complexion. I found Papa's loving manners comforting, especially as a young girl. During Nana's drinking rampages, both Papa and I would seek refuge at Saint James Park. He would carry a rolled blanket under his arm and a brown-bagged bottle of Thunderbird in his hand. We would sit at our usual bench; I with my head on his lap, comfortably covered while we waited it out. Every so often Papa would take a drink. Sitting upright like a protective soldier, he watched over me until the wee hours of the morning before we returned home.

It was obvious that my grandparents had a thorn in their relationship. I never saw them touch, or sleep, or eat together. It was something I accepted as their way of life. I never thought to ask Nana about it, even when she cried, which she often did when she drank.

I thought perhaps Papa in his younger years had hurt her vulnerable, young heart or simply that Nana's unforgiving heart yearned for her mom, holding unto memories knowing she was never to see her again. I never learned the secret. Sadly enough, I could only assume.

Papa, on the other hand, was opposite of Nana. He enjoyed walking the neighborhood, wearing his flannel shirt, khaki pants, and hat. With his glasses resting on the bridge of his nose, he would spend hours making me toys from wood or from mud. He would mix dirt with water and add powdered laundry starch and sugar, then shape the pliable mud into different animals. Sitting next to my Papa, eagerly watching him focus on his masterpieces, we would agree which one we liked best. He would gently place them in the sun to dry. I enjoyed that time with Papa. He was my first hero. Neither one of my grandparents ever learned to write or speak English.

From my perspective as a child, life appeared simple, yet hectic. With the rooster's first crow, warmly nestled against Nana, I knew it was almost time to get up. She would sit at the edge of our small twin bed, rolling tobacco to enjoy her first cigarette. I watched her take a puff. As she exhaled, she coughed. It was a deep hacking cough, and I wondered why she smoked since it was such a struggle for her to breathe.

The first regiment for Papa was to make coffee. When the aroma filled our little wood house on stilts, it was time for me to get up. I would sit next to Papa, wrapped in a blanket, while he carefully broke stale French bread into small bites, dropped them into a bowl filled with coffee and canned milk, topped with sugar and cinnamon. That was my breakfast. He made sure I ate before the long day ahead of us. While I ate, Nana would be over at the wood-burning potbelly stove, making tortillas stuffed with fried potatoes mixed with refried beans for our lunch.

Like clockwork, the big old truck with a half-torn canvas rumbled up our dead-end road to pick us up: the waiting men, women and children. The mornings were brisk, the women speaking in Spanish, saying, "Hurry up. Get in!" cramming us children toward the back so we could huddle together to keep warm. It was a long haul from our rural neighborhood in east San Jose to the massive, open fields, filled with a crop that was ripe and ready for picking. The days were long and hard for the adults, but for us kids, it was a time to play in our vast playground. (During cotton season, Papa would fill the huge canvas tote bag with cotton, and I would ride on top as he lugged the over-stuffed bag to the collecting bin.)

Everyone was weary at the end of the long workday. On the ride home, some would sleep, while others complained about their aches and pains that came from bending over all day. The highlight of the return trip was when old man Carlos or his wife Maria would break out in song, singing old Mexican folk songs they sang while working in the fields.

We kids would laugh and squirm. We often played a game of tag that, given the cramped space, amounted to little more than hitting each other and bumping into exhausted, motionless men and women. Out of nowhere, someone would slap us, yelling, "*Quedarse quieto!*" (Keep still!). Once we arrived at our stop, everyone would call out, "*Adios, hasta mañana*" (God bless until the morning), as we headed for our respective little houses.

At Nana's house, we were on our own to get our meals. Sometimes Papa would heat something up. We knew where to find the extra tortillas, wrapped in a cloth. We either made a burrito or put the food on our plate. We never used silverware. We scooped up the food with the tortillas. At dusk, the families would gather with the neighbors to play music around a bonfire. While Nana sat in her favorite chair on the porch and Papa mixed with the men, someone would begin singing, while another played the guitar or accordion. Because we had no ball or bat, we kids played "kick the can," kicking up a dust cloud from the dirt road—we could always find an empty beer can.

The weekends on Summer Street were great. At dusk, the men gathered wood for a fire in the middle of the road. The old people would set their chairs close to the fire to keep warm; there was always one who had a stick ready to hit us kids if we got too close to the fire. People would sing to the strumming guitars and accordion. The fire would crackle and pop, sending sparks up into the night sky. The men would start talking louder and louder, especially after a few beers, and the women would cluster together to gossip, giggling like little girls. It was a good life, simple and secure.

On Sundays, we would hear about God while sitting outside on wooden benches. Afterwards, the Franciscan priests would play kickball with us kids in the fields behind the church. It was funny to see them trying to run, stumbling in what looked like a long housecoat with a rope tied around their waists. They also laughed at their own clumsiness as they did their best to play with us. When we said something in Spanish, they encouraged us to speak in English even though they understood far more than they pretended.

The nuns, on the other hand, never smiled or played with us. We kids would wonder if they had hair under their big head coverings that matched their cloaks. If we spoke aloud or laughed out of order, Sister Beatrice, who had the biggest ruler compared to the other nuns, would appear from out of nowhere and smack us. This was especially true during catechism.

As a little girl, I knew no boundaries. I enjoyed exploring, but I knew to never go past the cow pasture to the housing development on the other side. One late afternoon, Nana went to bed early and Papa was already asleep, I amused myself by throwing rocks at the outhouse "toilet" door. I couldn't wait for Nana to fall asleep after reciting the rosary, which seemed like forever, so I could go out exploring.

But it was not to be. Nana opened the window and yelled at me in Spanish, "Stop making so much noise! You're scaring the chickens! And don't you dare leave. You stay away from *those* people!" She slammed the window shut. I could not imagine what made *those* people so bad when they appeared to live better then we did. Now I was more curious than ever.

My first glimpse of "those" kids was in kindergarten at Mayfair Elementary School. We were known as the "brown kids." My small group of friends sat outside at our favorite wooden table and bench, eating lunches that consisted of tomatoes and mayonnaise on Wonder Bread or a burrito wrapped in paper bags or cloths the size of dishtowels. I noticed that the little girls from the new housing development wore pretty dresses, had ribbons in their hair, and had lunch pails. Some of the girls placed a napkin on their lap as they delicately ate their half cut sandwich. I could not help but stare at them, wondering how they could be so bad, when they looked so nice and friendly. I wanted to find out and learn from them. I wondered why Nana resented them.

One evening after my grandparents had their usual drinks and went to bed early, my curiosity got the best of me. I snuck out of the house, crossed the cow pasture, carefully climbed the wooden fence, and peeked into one of the houses that didn't sit on stilts. To my surprise, I saw a picture-perfect family seated together at a kitchen table. The mom, the dad, the son, and the daughter were all nicely dressed. On the cloth-covered table were bowls filled with hot food. The mom served the kids first, and after that, the dad and mom served themselves. They all held hands and bowed their heads. That made no sense to me. During the meal, they talked and laughed, each adding to the conversation. I was confused; if that was bad for me then without a doubt I wanted to understand why. The experience left a deep imprint on my mind and a deep yearning for a connection, family time, communication, and respect; all of which were absent in my own family. This imprint became my core values.

"I asked God to grant me patience. And God said, 'No.' He said patience is the by-product of trials. It isn't granted; it is earned" - **Bob Baker**

Dad—A Little Girl's First Love

Sometimes my sister, brother and I stayed with Mom and Dad. When we did, we knew not to get too comfortable, knowing a fight was a common occurrence, especially after Dad started drinking. Eventually Sylvia and Robert stayed more with their friends or our grandparents to avoid the chaos of our parents. Being the youngest, my choices were limited. However, I had something that no one else had. When Mom left for work, I had Dad all to myself.

Dad was tall, dark and handsome, with the exception of his boxer's nose. As soon as Mom left in her mad dash to get to work, Dad would scoop me up, as if I was feather light, put me in the car, and drive to the downtown civic auditorium to watch the boxing matches.

As a frustrated former middleweight, professional boxer, Dad had hung up his gloves after I was born, but his desire for boxing never left him. Held in Dad's arms, I could sense the change in his personality as we entered the large, smoked-filled auditorium. He was in his element. The ring gave him a sense of significance and empowerment.

The regulars all knew each other, of course. Some clustered together, setting their bets, while others paced around with cigarettes hanging off their lips, talking intensely all the while, until they fitted themselves into position before the first fight.

Dad darted toward his usual foldout chair behind the ringside bell. I automatically sat onto his lap. Once the boxing matches started, he would move me to the chair next to him. The room was filled to capacity and the energy was electric and invigorating. Dad stood with the other spectators, fully engaged, yelling and swinging his fists as sweat from the boxers splattered across the gallery, sometimes spraying me.

The sounds at countdown were intense. I knew not to wander off and lose sight of Dad, especially during the final round when things got crazy. The crowd could get aggressive over their wins or losses. When the place emptied out after the final fight, many would grumble their disappointment.

"The lousy, stikin' bum," I'd hear as we passed by.

"Rigged, I tell ya, s'rigged," a man growled, clenching his fists.

"It's gone. All gone. I'm done fer!" These desperate words scared me, and I would hang on tight to Dad as we went out into the night.

It was a given that Dad and his cronies would meet up at the Ringside, a bar on First Street. Holding me high in his strong arms, he sauntered to his usual spot at the back of the room. The maroon-colored walls were covered with boxing memorabilia and black and white photos of famed boxers: Jack Dempsey, Young Herman, and Joe Lewis. The air stunk of stale beer and smoke. Men competed for

position, interrupting and talking over each other in a crazy, tumultuous show of male bonding.

"How'dja like that right jab! Knocked him on his ass," one would say.

"Awww, that was nothin'," a defender would respond. "He takes
worse 'n that 'fore he gets out o' bed in the mornin'."

Each one had a better version, jabbing each other, as if they were in
the ring, laughing as their cigarettes hung off their lips.

Holding me tight in one arm with his foot partially cradling a bar
stool, Dad was able to drink and smoke at the same time. Every once
in a while, he would assure me that we would go home soon. The
place was standing room only. Dad, boasting, attempting to make his
point of the moment, would absent-mindedly set me down on the
floor. I hugged one of his legs and nestled myself on his right foot
while his other foot was anchored to the barstool. Even in the midst
of this drunken chaos, Dad maintained an awareness that if he failed
to get us back before Mom got home; he was in for a hell of a fight.

Dad's story to his friends was always the same: "You wait, one day I'll
own my own bar." Due to his proclivity toward self-delusion, no one
ever took him seriously. His friends teased him about his unfulfilled
dreams.

But, Dad was right. The bar across the street from our house went
into receivership, and Dad struck a deal for it. On the day he opened
the bar, many of his friends from the Ringside came to celebrate his
victory. Everyone was happy. I remember people dancing to the music blasting from his prized jukebox, clutching their beer bottles in
their hands.

Mom quit her job as a waitress to help Dad with the bar. They both
appeared happy as they busied themselves making sure the patrons
enjoyed themselves. While my parents worked, I curled up with a
blanket under the cash register in two big empty beer boxes, which
Dad had made into a bed for me.

Many of the patrons started tabs, which Dad openly accepted, ignoring Mom's pointed expression of disapproval. It was his dream, and he didn't want to spoil it. Dad lived his dream, but not for long. One day two men removed the jukebox and loaded it onto the bed of their pickup truck. Dad followed them outside, making furious gestures.

"Hold on there, you guys! "Gotta have a little patience! I'll pay you!" he yelled out. I was afraid for him. He sounded scared.

Little by little, people stopped coming to the bar. It wasn't long before the dream came to a screeching halt. Dad's commitment to fulfilling his dream had apparently known no bounds. Unbeknown to Mom, he had conspired with Uncle David, a professional swindler, to steal the trust deed to Nana's house. My sister and brother had gone to live there until Mom and Dad settled down. It was short lived. Dad had forged Nana's "X" signature and sold it. That was how he had raised the money to buy the bar.

All hell broke loose when the bank repossessed Nana's little wooden house and she was evicted. That was a sad day. As I recall, Nana's eviction happened around the same time that the bar closed down. Dad underwent a drastic change. He stopped spending time with me. Every time I assured him everything was going to be all right he would push me away, but I hung out near him in our small one bedroom house.

Consumed by darkness, Dad was unable to see his way out of the repercussions of his destructive decisions. Mom got a job right away. As she left for work in the mornings, Dad would prop himself up comfortably on the overstuffed living room sofa and drink. I would make every effort to get his attention, but to no avail; he would not say a word, just nudge me to leave him alone while he drank.

His drinking became excessive. Obviously ashamed, he would hide his bottle in a brown paper bag. During that time, he became more physically abusive to Mom. The sounds of their fighting horrified me. I distracted myself by looking up into a hole in the bedroom ceiling, where a mouse would periodically peak down at me.

Dad's fear of being ostracized for losing the bar kept him away from the Ringside and his friends. Gambling took its toll, too. He eventually ran out of items to sell to support his habits—like the television set and the bicycles he bought us kids for Christmas.

Dad's nature to live spontaneously predicted his final departure. He left without saying goodbye to me. Mom acted as if nothing had happened—out of sight, out of mind—and never mentioned him again after he left. I missed him terribly. I tenaciously held onto my memories of our fun times together. I believed that if Mom had tried harder to keep Dad happy, he would not have left us. I believed that one day he would return to me after all I was his princess, dads little girl.

"Fear constricts - Love expands"

Will I Become Like Mommy?

After Dad left, my family and I moved into a small apartment that required Mom to work two jobs. My brother Robert's unfulfilled desire for Dad's attention created a void in his life that led him into a destructive street life. At age 13, he was taken in to live with a neighborhood woman twice his age who gave birth to his first son. My sister Silvia ran away and married her first boyfriend, George, in pursuit of happiness. That became a nightmare because he turned out to be a drug dealer.

My sister just like Mom had hoped to find Prince Charming, someone who would sweep them off their feet and provide a loving, secure way of life. A life that was way beyond working in the fields which Mom had been accustomed to as a child. I could understand the attraction my parents had for each other and their common desire to leave behind their parent's life of drudgery.

I missed my Dad very much. Still holding on to him emotionally, I decided to find him. I asked the phone operator to connect me to Santa Claus in hopes he knew where my dad was. The operator laughed and thought my request was cute. She suggested I talk to my mom.

I was so frustrated. I wasn't trying to be cute. I wanted answers regarding my dad's whereabouts. Time passed. One day I noticed Mom clenching the phone bill in her hand, unaware that it revealed my disappointing phone call to Santa. She scared me. Furious, she railed at me.

"That's it! I'm sick of it! You think he's so great! You want to see him? Do you"? This fantasy of yours is coming to an end, once and for all. You're coming with me. Then you'll see. Then you'll know who your Dad is!"

She grabbed my arm, dragged me out of the house, and pushed me into the car. She drove for what seemed like forever. Terrified, I didn't dare move or speak. I felt sick to my stomach, but nothing could have prepared me for the unimaginable shock that was waiting for me.

We entered the grounds of Agnews State Mental Hospital in Milpitas. She directed me to get out of the car. Mom hastily walked across the yard, with her handbag securely clutched as she stomped on the wet grass leaving indentations with each step. I followed behind her towards a large two story unassuming building that had a meshed wrought iron fence and huge windows. All I could see were nurses in white uniforms and strange looking people walking around the enclosure. Then I saw the figure of a broken, frail man walking towards us.

"*How's my girl?*" he said in a faint, hollow voice.

I barely recognized my dad, stunned I stood back. I couldn't speak. Mom and Dad had a few words while I stood in disbelief, wondering what had happened to him. Could this really be daddy? I looked at him and felt hopeless, knowing I would not be able to offer him comforting words of assurance. Mom was right: that experience put an end to my search for my father.

We left the hospital grounds with Mom driving, emotionless, without any explanation. The experience completed that chapter in my life with Dad. Still, I felt that our separation connected us vicariously because now we were both lonely with shattered dreams.

The small place Mom and I shared felt big because Mom was seldom home. She had two jobs: during the day, she worked in the cannery and at night, she worked at a nightclub. When she arrived home from her day job, she always looked exhausted and smelled like sulfur. She wore a fruit-stained covered apron, a net in her hair, and no make-up.

After Mom's bath and make-up ritual, she would transform into a beautiful woman. It was obvious she enjoyed her job selling cigarettes while wearing a cute outfit at the Grand Majestic nightclub. When it was time for her to apply her make-up, I eagerly sat at the edge of the bed to watch her. It was like watching an artist meticulously apply vivid colors to a flawless light complexion while enjoying a cup of coffee and smoking a cigarette. I knew each step of the process all the way to the final touch. I regretfully watched Mom puckering her lips to apply her favorite boysenberry Revlon lipstick. That meant it was almost time for her to leave. Knowing her ritual, one night I hid her lipstick in hopes I would make her late for work. To my surprise, she knew what I was up to and angrily said, "WHATS WRONG!" with you?" as she raised her hand as if to slap me. I immediately ducked and retrieved her lipstick and played it off as if I had suddenly found it.

I liked it when she did not work at night and was home with me; but even then, not much changed. She kept to herself most of the time, sitting on the living room sofa with her arms crossed, periodically taking a puff from her cigarette, gazing out the living room window.

The partially rolled up window blinds kept the room dim. Mom sat for hours, absorbed by her thoughts; thoughts she never shared with me.

Before Mom went to work at night, she would warn me to stay home, keep the lights off except for one lamp, and not to open the door for anyone. Before she left for her morning job, her strict instruction was always the same: "If a social worker unexpectedly drops by, don't tell her I am working."

After Mom left, I would sometimes venture out and visit my hobo friends. They camped at the railroad's boxcar transfer station not far from our apartment. One morning, I hopped on a train. It was thrilling, yet I did not know the next stop was in Santa Clara, several miles away getting back home, felt like forever.

A few hobos gathered at their usual camp at dusk and allowed me join them near the fire pit. The warmth of the fire felt good, especially when it was damp and cold. As I sat on an upside down coffee can, I watched as each man took up a task to prepare their shared meal. Their unwashed wool, body odor, tobacco smoke, and cooking yielded an unpleasant smell. I knew it was time to leave when the men started drinking and saying bad words.

One evening on my way to the campsite, Jigger, the "friendly one," popped out from tall bushes and startled me. He looked at me with an unfamiliar expression on his face and threw a rock at me, barely missing.

"Go away!," he said with a whispery, raspy voice. "Go away, yu hear! Get the heck out of here! And never come back or else!" with his hand raised signaling me to hurry.

He was not angry, but the expression on his face scared me enough so that I never returned. When I looked back, I knew it was time for me to move on because his face did not match his actions. What I saw in him was a protective concern.

I was now 11. It was a difficult time for me because I did not understand the changes within my body. My emotions erupted for no reason. I began to isolate myself by staying in my apartment and watching television, eating canned spaghetti and canned corn. I will never forget my introduction to feminine hygiene. One morning on the front porch, I noticed a small item wrapped in a brown paper bag with my name on it. To my great humiliation, it was deodorant. It was obvious to somebody that I needed help.

The first experience I had with my menstrual cycle was similar to the movie *Carrie*. Having no concept of a period, I believed I was dying. I ran home from school, wrote Mom a note on a paper bag that I loved her, using her dark brown eyebrow pencil, and then hid in the back shed to meet my death. I fell asleep. I was startled awake, hearing my mom and sister calling my name. When I walked out of the shed, Mom was standing there, looking angry. When we walked back into the apartment, she spat at my sister, saying, "tell her what to do!" It was obvious from her tone that I had much to learn, but it was not going to come from her.

My favorite pastime at night was peeking out of my bedroom window when all the lights were off. The window shade was pulled down, but from the corner I could peek at the neighbors next door. I was intrigued. They were always doing something. I was most amazed how 13 people, all belonging to the same family, could live in a two-bedroom apartment. Music was always blasting from their place, cars would come and go at all hours, and the women were always barefoot. I wondered if their calloused feet hurt.

I was fascinated with how these women washed clothes in a washbasin on a scrub board, using what appeared to be a medium-sized rock, and how they hung blankets over a rope line and whacked at them with a broom. The doors and windows were seldom closed—an open invitation for anyone to go in or out. I was especially attracted to the young boy who attended junior high and wore a leather jacket that made him look cool. I could not wait to get out of elementary school so that I could attend the same school as him. Little did I realize at the time that this boy would become one of the biggest turning points in my life.

The first month of junior high felt awkward, especially at the first school dance. The popular girls gathered and giggled while the boys asked them to dance. Closest to the doors sat the unpopular, awkward group where Hazel, my neighbor friend with long, curly copper red hair, and I sat. At that time, I was an awkward, clumsy girl, always looking down at my terribly pigeon-toed feet.

One day on my way to school, Hazel was riding in a car with three boys. They stopped and asked if I wanted a ride. Just as I was getting into the back seat, an unusual feeling came over me. It was as if something was telling me not to get into the car. I stepped back out and told them no. They laughed and sped off. The next day on my way to school, as I passed the corner grocery store, I noticed the Mercury News headlines stating in bold print: "Teenaged Kids Killed." The article described how they had driven off the road in the Santa Cruz Mountains.

Stunned in disbelief, still hearing Hazel's seldom heard laughter in my mind, I was overcome with sadness. I was scared at how close I had come to making the wrong decision. The kids who gossiped, teased, and made fun of Hazel's hair and eyebrows that connected as one brow, suddenly began talking to me, asking questions about her. They didn't care about her. They were just nosey. I learned quickly that I could not trust them and kept to myself.

It was obvious that I had a crush on Bobby, the boy next door. All he had to do was look at me and my heart fluttered. One late afternoon, Bobby saw me standing in front of my yard carving my initials on the tree and he came over and added his initials next to mine. After that, I was his, especially when he unexpectedly kissed me before leaving with his buddies who drove up to get him. I was ecstatic. Unfortunately, at school he ignored me; in fact, he sometimes made fun of me while being with his friends.

One day as I was walking home from school, Bobby pulled up next to me in a slick two-door coupe. I could hear deejay Wolfman Jack and the music blaring on the radio. He asked if I wanted a ride home. In a split second, my fear of Mom was overruled by an intense excitement for Bobby. I got into his car. Instead of driving me home, we cruised around. We drove about 20 miles to his Aunt Mary's house. When we arrived, she was standing outside, angry. She said that the car was stolen and began scolding both Bobby and me. I had been completely unaware that Bobby had stolen the car, and hearing how angry she was, I became terrified of what Mom was going to do to me.

It was too late to go back home, but Bobby's Aunt Mary assured me that in the morning she would take me. She called my mom but there was no answer. Bobby acted as if nothing had happened. He took me into the back room and began kissing me. He was rough and his kissing hurt. He pushed me down and I became frightened. Fortunately, his aunt called out and he stopped. Bobby's friends picked him up to go out and he did not return that night. He didn't care that he left me crying, feeling ashamed and scared of what had almost happened. All I wanted to do was to go home, face the consequences from Mom, crawl into my bed, and cry. I was so embarrassed.

I didn't know how to make sense of my feelings. I had such a crush on Bobby. When he attempted to force himself on me, it was terrifying, exciting, and confusing, all at the same time. It filled me with shame, but at the same time, I expected it because that was how Dad treated Mom. At 14, my emotions ruled, distorting my need to be loved. I felt it was inevitable, like waiting in line to get on the scariest amusement park ride ever; the closer I came to getting on the ride, the more fear and excitement meshed together. My young, vulnerable heart had no concept of the consequences; I only saw the possibility of being loved, of filling the void that Dad left in my heart.

Little did I know that Mom's need for love and her loneliness was even greater than my own. I never expected what faced me ahead.

"People don't reach their full potential because they seek purpose and don't know how"

Chapter Two: Depleted

Robbed of Innocence

The following morning, Bobby's Aunt Mary drove me back to his house. Bobby's mom, Juana, was waiting outside for our arrival. Like the changing of the guards, Mary entered the house and Juana escorted me home next door. I was fidgety and could not wait to get inside my apartment to welcome a beating and rant from Mom.

Walking up the steps, I noticed through the screen that the door was open. I stood behind Juana. Suddenly, I saw Mom approach the screen door. I moved forward, expecting the door to open. What followed was unbelievably surreal: Mom stood behind the screen and with one hand on the door said, "*Keep her!*" and then "*firmly*" closed the door.

"I was stunned and went numb!" I questioned to myself "What happened?" Mom just closed the door in my face without hesitation, just like I had seen her do so many times to door-to-door salesmen. Juana and I stood in shock, still looking at the closed door in "disbelief" not comprehending what Mom had meant by "keep her." Juana and I walked back to her place, not saying a word; I walked behind her with my arms crossed and looking down, feeling drained each step took an effort. Before entering, I glanced at the window from where I had so often peaked out from, in curiosity and within a split second I realized that the life I viewed from that window was my new reality. As I stepped inside their house, I felt an overwhelming sense of sadness. Just the day before I was in school, just another normal day, and now, much like my dad, I was rejected and would soon be forgotten. With 13 people living in a two-bedroom house, I became the 14th person. All of a sudden, still unable to comprehend, I knew my life had changed forever.

She pointed out a spot for me to sit. I watched as she moved a small mattress into a tiny dining room corner. She created a divider from neatly folded, mold smelling clothes, which they had collected to be dispersed on their annual trip to Mexico. After she finished, she said in a rough voice, that that was my bed from now on. I curled up onto the smelly bed, covered my face with old musty clothes and cried, trying to muffle the sounds, while everyone talked about what had happened to me.

That night after everyone had fallen asleep, Bobby returned home drunk, he obviously heard what had happened. He entered my cubicle and grabbed my shoulders, pressing me down. He said I belonged to him now, and that I had better not say anything. He hit me hard in my face and forced himself on me. From that time forward, he would hit me before having sex. The boy I thought was so cute had turned ugly. His abuse, especially after drinking, became a frequent nightmare.

I never returned to school and eventually gave up hope that Mom would take me back. At 14, I was abused on a regular basis, rejected and forgotten by my mother, and had no place to live, except my smelly sleeping cubicle. I accepted and surrendered to my fate.

I was not afraid of Bobby hitting me. I believed it was an expression of love because I used to hear my dad do it to my mom many times after they fought behind closed doors. I would hear Mom crying and Dad saying, "I love you, I'm sorry" However, even though Bobby hit me, he never said, "I love you; I figured that's why he was not sorry.

Living conditions in the two-bedroom house were filthy, with a mildewed, dirty sock smell that even Pine-Sol couldn't overcome. With seven adults, three teenagers, including myself, and three kids, every day at the house was chaotic. This was true especially at night when everyone rolled out their mattresses. Juana and her husband were kind to me, but turned a blind-eye to Bobby's abuse. Since my sleeping cubicle was near the kitchen, at night I could hear the sounds of huge rats chomping away on any food that was left out. Sometimes when I needed to use the bathroom near the kitchen, I would flip on the light and see hundreds of cockroaches running to hide.

Once, a huge pot of beans was left on the stove to cool down. As I walked into the kitchen, I saw a rat run across a shelf and fall, landing in the pot of hot beans. It screamed as it sank, then was silent. I was startled. That experience became my spiteful moment. I said nothing. The following morning, when the family scooped beans into their freshly made tortillas before going to work, I passed on that meal.

Despite all that, I noticed the women of the house worked hard and never complained as they attended to their men's needs. Juana showed me how to take care of Bobby. She showed me how to make starch from powder in a box to perfectly crease Bobby's khaki pants and iron his t-shirts and underwear. I also learned how to use the outside scrub board, washing the clothes with a bar of Lava soap.

When it was my day to wash, I would spend time looking at the window next door, dreaming that one day Mom would let me come home. Even if she was seldom there, at least her house was clean. Days turned into weeks and weeks turned into months, and after realizing my dream would never come true, the longing in my heart for Mom diminished and I accepted my fate as belonging to Bobby.

One day, Juana told me to put on a dress and informed me that I was going to see my mom. I was numb with shame but excited to see her again, hoping she would take me back. Juana drove Bobby and me to the courthouse and ushered us into a judge's chamber. Mom stood there, emotionless, with arms crossed. This so-called "reunion" was arranged by Mom to get us married, an experience we both were too young to understand. Ironically, after we were married, Bobby claimed his independence and spent most of his time hanging out with his gang-affiliated family. There would be times when he did not even come home.

One morning I awoke burning with fever. For days I laid motionless, feverish, chilled and soaked in pee, watching white bed bugs turn red, crawling all over me, fading in and out of consciousness. At a distance, I imagined a familiar voice calling my name. It was my sister, Silvia. I had not seen her since she ran away to marry George. According to Silvia, Mom had been checking up on me through her bedroom window. Normally, she would see me outside washing clothes or sitting on the porch watching the kids from school go by, but she had not seen me outside for days. She had grown concerned and called Silvia to check on me. I remember my sister carrying me out of that squalid hell-hole and taking me to County Hospital. I was admitted and diagnosed with double pneumonia—and pregnant.

My frail body was covered with bed bug bites. I had a very high fever. I had lost a lot of weight. The doctor explained that I might lose my baby. I was scared and alone. That night I shared a small room with an elderly lady who was very sick. She cried often, moaning in pain. Even after a nurse settled her down with medication, within a short time she would begin crying for help. One night I heard her talking in a soft, welcoming tone to someone. I knew no one else was in the room with us but sensed something different. Her voice was clear, peaceful, and without agonizing pain. After a short pause, she made an unfamiliar gurgling sound and became quiet. The next morning, the nurse found her dead.

That experience left a big impression on me, a desire to understand who or what brought her such peace when she was obviously hurting so much. I thought how lucky she was to find resolution. After a week, they released me from the hospital. Juana picked me up and drove straight to the Welfare Office to sign me up. I was familiar with the place because I often went there with Mom. The social worker asked me for my mother's phone number to verify needed information. I was eager to hear Mom's voice, but her phone had been disconnected. She had moved away. I was crushed.

I continued living with Bobby's family even though he had started another family down the street. He came home to change clothes to go out at night and like clockwork made monthly visits to take most of my welfare check from his mom, since I was a minor. After my son, Danny, was born, life had purpose for me. Most of my time was spent between Bobby's mom and Nana's house, learning how to care for my precious baby boy. That's when I began to see Mom again with her new born son, now my step brother who was only three months older then Danny. She seemed happier than I'd ever seen her. My grandma's house became Grand Central Baby Station because my sister, with her firstborn baby girl, also visited. Life seemed somewhat settled now. Bobby visited once a week, usually when he was drunk, to have sex with me, and again I became pregnant, giving birth to my little girl, Sandi nine months later.

One night, when I was bored, I decided to find my brother. I left both babies with Juana at her bedside, sleeping soundly. I knew he hung out with druggies at an abandoned garage. It was near a creek under the railroad tracks. I walked through the empty streets. The night was cold and foggy. When I arrived at the musty, broken-down, garage, it was empty, except for an old mildewed mattress that lay on the dirt floor. A cold wind was blowing and the fog was rolling in through a missing window. I got scared, curled up on the mattress and fell asleep.

Suddenly I awoke to the sound of men; one voice I recognized as my brother Robert. All he said was, "Hey, sis," like this had been a regular occurrence. He did not seem surprised to see me. His focus was on preparing his arm to shoot up. The other guy, with a steady, surgeon-like hand, masterly held the heroin powder-filled spoon in one hand, while in the other held a cigarette lighter under it. They all had their eyes focused on the flame. No one spoke. The other guy was already smacked out, with a lopsided smile on his face. Then it was Robert's turn.

I was amazed to see him fade off into a surrendering bliss, which caught my attention. I immediately sat up and extended my arm to the last man, named Frank, who was frantically looking for an acceptable vein. I said to him, "Please, I want that."

This weathered, hunched over, frail man, covered with old track scars, paused and stared at me. He looked right into my soul and said, "No. "God has plans for you." Those words flowed clearly and fluidly from his mouth. He turned away, found a vein, and joined the others in the abyss.

I wondered what it meant, especially from the mouth of an addict, who despite his lethargic mannerisms spoke words that were bold and direct. I was perplexed. *God? Plans? What plans?* "I could not comprehend it". I didn't even know God was there. How could he know who I was among all the millions of people in the world? Even though I didn't understand, it was the first time I had heard that God was personal or that he had plans for me. I got up and returned home feeling rejected and discouraged.

It was right after delivering third baby, my son Paul, who surprised us by coming while we were at a drive-in theater (the only time Bobby was actually with me at a delivery), that I decided it was time to leave Juana's house. I did not want my children to be raised in that filthy house, and I was desperate to get away from Bobby. I went to the Welfare Office and they agreed to assign my check directly to a landlord. As a result, I was finally able to rent a small, one-bedroom, unfurnished duplex with a refrigerator and stove. I bought a twin mattress and a crib at a garage sale for my three babies and me.

The happiness of being on my own soon turned into a terrible, aching loneliness. I would sit on the front porch with the kids for hours, hoping someone would pass by and stop to talk to me, even though I was shy and ashamed of being uneducated and abused. I felt stupid. When someone spoke to me, I would mumble. I felt worthless and unable to articulate my thoughts and feelings. I lived mostly in my head and talked to myself.

I never learned to cook. The only thing I knew how to do was to make fresh tortillas, boil beans, and steam rice, adding catsup or sugar with condensed milk on the rice for variety. Because the pneumonia had left me frail and unhealthy, I was not able to breast-feed my baby, and I was unable to afford baby formula. I learned to improvise, using water from boiled beans and rice mixed with corn syrup, and at times, condensed milk.

Diapers were a luxury I couldn't afford. I stole a bed sheet from my neighbor's clothing line to make diapers. I knew it was not right, but sometimes stealing a loaf of bread from an early delivery left at the corner grocery store was essential for me to feed my babies when I ran out of flour to make tortillas. I loved when my neighbor baked raisin oatmeal cookies—my favorite—and the smell would permeate through our common wall and fill my little place. I would wait patiently in the early morning for her to leave for work, then sneak into her duplex through a laundry-room common window, and take a cookie from her refrigerator. A part of me wondered if she had baked those cookies for me. She never questioned or confronted me about the missing cookies.

The days were long and boring; the nights lonely and restless, always keeping a watchful eye out for the rats that would climb up my babies' crib while they were sleeping. The fear of rats biting them required resourcefulness. I tied a piece of string around the crib with numerous small Christmas bells attached to wake me up during the night when the rats came out. The sound of the bells would frighten them away.

My husband, Bobby, would still show up unexpectedly for a few hours, which were better than dealing with the unbearable loneliness. Thoughts of suicide began to consume me. My first thought was who would care for my kids, and in my simple-mindedness I believed my neighbor, who baked those delicious oatmeal raisin cookies, kept a clean house, and always had a smile on her face, would care for and raise them.

Planning my demise gave me a false sense of purpose because I felt I could at least do that successfully. My first attempt was to lie on the nearby train tracks after dark so that the train would not stop and run me over. I fed my babies and made sure they were asleep before walking to the tracks to end my misery. I had timed the train for days and it was never late in arriving at my chosen spot. I arrived ten minutes before the train was set to pass by. I lay down on the tracks. It felt like I had lain there forever, but the train never came. I got up, defeated, and went home to my babies.

A few days passed, and I tried to keep things together, but the loneliness was too much to bear. I decided on Plan B, which was to fill my small kitchen with gas from the little four-burner stove and die of suffocation. I fed my babies and rocked each of them to sleep, gently placing them together in their shared crib. I rolled the crib out to the common enclosed porch I began to carefully with masking tape seal the doors and windows in the kitchen. Overcome with immense sadness I turned on the gas and cried myself to sleep while thinking of my poor babies, believing they were better off without me and that someone else would give them a better life then I could.

I woke up with a horrible headache and could hear them crying. Removing the masking tape from the door, I found the kids still in their crib unable to climb out. The one- and two-year-olds, Danny and Sandi, were standing up shaking the crib, happy to see me, while Baby Paul slept soundly. I eagerly picked them up, happy to hold them again. I took the kids to the front porch to play while I aired out the apartment. Still feeling lightheaded with a severe headache, holding Paul in my arms and keeping the other kids from stepping off the porch, I noticed a bright orange tag wired to the gas meter. It read, "Gas turned off due to lack of payment." I couldn't believe it. *"It was a miracle!*

I couldn't stop crying, loving on my precious babies, hugging and holding them tightly even as they squirmed out from under my arms to play. I could not take my eyes off them. I felt so guilty, consumed with sorrow, when a terrifying thought hit me—*"what if I had succeeded and died"*. That meant, at this moment my babies would have still been in their crib, crying, all alone, abandoned with no one to give them comfort.

My heart began pounding, and then suddenly, in horror, I envisioned my soul floating above them. I saw my dead body on the floor. I could hear myself crying, "I'm so sorry," pleading, "Someone help them," calling my babies' names. As I faded away, with my babies' helpless cries ringing in my ears, "mommy, mommy" . . . "That monumental revelation was "pure hell". The pain was unforgettably intense and gave me a clear perspective on the value of life. With a renewed sense of hope, I felt everything was going to be all right.

Because my utilities were shut off and I had no money or food, I had no choice but to ask Nana if my babies and I could move in with her. When she said yes, I sighed deeply with relief. My kids gave me a reason to function daily, but not enough to believe in my self or my potential. I didn't realize then that my weakness was equal to my strength, waiting to be discovered. GPS was watching over me, waiting for me to wake up from sleep and ignite my internal spark into a burning flame.

"A person can never out-perform their own self-image"

Chapter Three: Damned

Dating the Devil

My suicide attempts came from a false belief that my kids would be better off without me, and that I would be sparing them from suffering. Because I had no positive family connection, I was frantic to fill the void of loneliness and stop the pain, even if it meant ending my life, or worse. Bobby's visits came further and further apart, but I still got pregnant. I was 18 years old when I gave birth to my fourth child, who was born prematurely and barely weighed four pounds.

Shortly after I recovered from his birth, I left the kids with my grandparents while I worked at a Mexican restaurant a few blocks away. I enjoyed the work, particularly interacting with adults, which I had missed so much. It is no wonder that when another man came into my life, I was desperate to feel loved and wanted.

I saw him park his Harley motorcycle in front of the restaurant. He was a tall and muscular guy with a chiseled jaw, black hair, and weathered skin. He had an authoritative presence and his tough appearance was intense. He walked in, sat at the counter, took off his leather jacket, and sported a pack of Marlboro cigarettes, tucked under the short sleeve of his t-shirt. He lit a cigarette and ordered a beer. Because I was still a minor at the time, another waitress served him. He drank several beers with his meal. Before leaving, he looked at me, and asked what time I got off work. I stumbled over my words, shocked that he noticed me. He said goodbye and took off.

Hours later, to my surprise, he showed up again. When he parked his Harley, he motioned to me to get on his bike, eyes convincingly demanding. Overjoyed and enraptured, I got on his Harley and took off with this man named Jack. Though I felt what I was doing was wrong, I held on to him because there was something about Jack that was exciting and forbidden. I was like a mouse baited by cheese in a trap, under the wire, surrendering my life to be close to the cheese.

We rode in the warm California evening. It was a lot of fun and I thought I had found my first friend. We drove to a huge Victorian-era, two-story house with a wrap-around porch and a neglected lawn. There were men sitting on the porch, smoking and looking at us. Some of the outside windows were covered with newspapers or aluminum foil.

Jack and I entered the house from the laundry room it was dark inside with a stale stench that reaped throughout. The kitchen was large with wall to wall cabinets, each had locks with respective owner names in black bold ink. Jack hurriedly led me to his extremely small cigarette smoked filled room and gave me a beer, which I did not like the taste. And then he gave me a "black beauty" pill, he said would take the edge off; I didn't remember much of anything after that. The next thing I knew I was walking to my grandparent's house later that night. One day Jack picked me up after work to show me where he moved too. The 3 room sparely furnished wooden house had a huge unkempt yard with a half tilted detached garage. His neighbors were far in between. The setting was perfect for his pastime entertainment which was training dogs to become vicious. He used live rabbits as bait as they squirmed to be free, Jack then released them to run for their lives from the slobbering Rottweiler's chase. The sounds they made were horrendous and terrifying. Jack thought it was funny; only sometimes a rabbit made it through a crack in the fence and escaped into the open fields. It was getting late, I decided to show him that I could cook and have dinner before heading home. I boiled some cabbage to eat with the hot pot of beans he had on the stove. Jack walked into the kitchen for a can of beer and went ballistic.

"What da hell's wrong with you? "Yu stupid idiot"! "Yu done! Stunk up, dis- whole f.... place!" He stomped towards me. His fury frightened me. I quickly reached over to remove the boiling pot from the stove. Jack shoved me aside, grabbed both pots, and threw them onto the floor. They bounced on the wooden floor, splattering cabbage, broth, and beans all over the kitchen, including the walls. The boiling mess barely missed me my legs.

Jack stomped outside, still spouting hateful words, calling me disgusting names, and yelled, "Yu bed-ha" clean this f.... mess and get the "hell" "ou-dha" my face" yu stupid "B...." before I get back!" He got on his Harley and headed for the local bar. It took me forever to clean up the mess. By the time I finished, it was dark outside. Exhausted, I got on the bus, went to my grandparent's house to pick up the kids, and finally made it home. At least he hadn't hit me, but I was shaken up.

Bobby's periodic nightly visits had almost ended, and I was spared from his physical abuse. I had not seen Jack for over a week. I was missing him so much. It consumed me. It was a lot like feeling drug withdrawals. I needed a fix. I needed Jack. Unexpectedly, one night after putting the kids to sleep, I heard Jack's motorcycle in front of my house. I raced out to invite him in. He sat on his bike, leaning on one foot, with the motor still running.

"Bitch, Im finished with you," he snarled, pointing at me. "The ex-wife is visiting from Texas, so stay away, "yu scuz!" Then he drove off.

His rejection devastated me. I couldn't believe he was finished with me. I couldn't get him out of my mind. A week went by and my addiction to Jack was at its peak. "I needed my fix!" "I needed Jack". I decided to pay him a surprise visit. I left the kids with a neighbor, knowing they were safe with her. I quickly put on a pretty, paisley print dress, did my hair in a ponytail, and took a bus across town. The closer the bus came to Jack, the more anxious I became. I finally got off the bus and walked several blocks to his house, with my heart beating with fear, anticipation, and excitement. Soon I would see him. Soon he would love me again.

When I was a block away, out of nowhere, a lady came up to me and stopped me by putting one hand on my shoulder. She pointed her finger at me and simply said, "God wants you." I first thought, "I don't want God, I want Jack!" Then, with a jolt, I realized her words were like the words Frank, the heroin addict, had spoken to me— the words that still echoed in my mind: "*God has plans for you*". Now, a complete stranger, an old lady, was telling me the same thing. It made absolutely no sense. Why would God want a no-body like me? I noticed the lady's deep wrinkles. She was old and crazy, but there was something about her. She spoke with loving concern. Then she turned around and walked away. The closer to Jacks house I had a strange feeling in the pit of my stomach. I knew I needed to return home, but at the same time, my destructive, toxic obsession over-ruled. My need was greater than my reason I was determined to see him.

I reached the front door and Jack opened it abruptly, as if he had been expecting me. With a beer in one hand, he pulled me in with the other. He pushed me to the couch and ordered me to watch him as he teased his dogs. He threw what could only have been a large, skinned rabbit towards them. I watched, horrified, as they tore the piece of meat apart. All around the house were empty beer cans, an empty whiskey bottle and cigarette butts piled on the large ashtray and thrown about the coffee table.

I realized I had willfully stepped into a pit of hell. I recalled the first time I got onto his bike and the forbidden feeling I had when I put my arms around his waist; I realized at that moment, it was the devil himself. His eyes were dilated and red, around his mouth was old dry saliva Jack looked unhuman. He instantly locked the front door with triple latches, grabbed me by my ponytail, and swung me towards the dogs like a skinned rabbit. They growled, but did not bite.

Jack dragged me by my hair and threw me on the bed. He bound and gagged me, and then commenced to do the unimaginable to my body. After what felt like hours he locked me in a small closet with his dogs. They sniffed around for a place to get comfortable and growled every time I moved. I stayed as stiff as possible, no longer bound, but still gagged. Jack was wild with drinking. He would only let me out of the closet to repeat his attacks on me with his dogs swirling around us, growling and salivating. He then again, locked me in the closet and I passed out.

By this point, I did not know if it was day or night. I remained in the closet, cold and wet because I had peed on myself. I heard Jack staggering towards the small bedroom where the dogs laid in front of the closet. As soon as he opened the door, he ripped the tape from my mouth. I begged him for water. As he turned to walk towards the kitchen, I found strength to get up, race to the front door, and tried frantically to unlock the latches. The door opened and I ran out into the empty street. It was pitch-dark outside. I could hear Jack running behind me. He grabbed my hair and dragged me back into his house. I tried to yell but no sound came out. I fought with all my might but was no match for his strength or his wrath.

Once I was back inside his house, Jack brutally attacked me again and when he was finished threw me into the closet. My body was bleeding all over. At one point, he was so angry and crazy that he grabbed his rifle and shoved it into my mouth. As I was gagging, he pulled the trigger. *Click.* I was not afraid of dying because my mind was numb. I welcomed death because of the pain. As he cocked his rifle again, I heard a police siren in the distance coming towards the house. Someone must have heard the commotion and called the police. He threw the rifle down, ran out, jumped on his motorcycle and sped off.

I lay in the closet with the door left open. My body was trembling from shock. A police officer walked in, picked me up in his arms, and carried me out. I don't remember him speaking to me. I only remember the smell and texture of his uniform as he carried me, my head leaning against his badge. He gently placed me in the front seat of his car. He drove me to the county hospital where I'd been many times when my babies were sick.

According to the doctor, I had cuts and bruises, a broken nose, a fractured arm, and my private area was severely lacerated. The kind, gentle policeman waited in the emergency room while I was patched up. I don't remember him asking me where he could drop me off or if I had family; it felt as if he already knew my situation. The policeman took me back to the car and proceeded to drive to a nice area of town. It was already morning when he stopped at a two-story house. My head was leaning on the window of his car as I watched him knock on the door. A woman answered and all I could see was her head moving side to side as if to say no.

He returned to the car and drove to Skid Row near the Greyhound Depot. It came to me that this policeman had no radio or sound in his car. There was a strange stillness in the car and I felt a deep peace of being safe and secure. He doubled parked and carried me as if I was a feather up a long flight of stairs. Cradled in his arms, I smelled his uniform and attempted to read his nametag, but could not endure the pain of moving my head. He spoke to the clerk behind a secured window and received the key to a room and a meal ticket for the Sun- Sun Chinese Restaurant below.

The long dark hallway was filled with cigarette smoke mixed with the sour smell of Chinese food. There were rooms on either side of the hall, with a common bathroom at the end. He carried me into a room. He placed me onto a single bed. His head knocked the light bulb dangling at the end of an electrical cord, hanging from the ceiling, causing it to sway.

Without saying a word, he gently closed the door behind him. I heard men's voices and coughing in the distance, but did not hear the policeman's steps going down the long corridor. I kept my eyes on the swaying light bulb and drifted into a deep sleep.

To this day, without any doubt in my mind, I believe he was an angelic being in human form dressed as a police officer who took care of me that frightful day. Angels in work clothes are God's helpers who carry out the assignments given to them by God; assignments to help souls who have forgotten they are children of God, our Father, "who always hears and knows our pain."

Despair

When I woke up, I could barely remember what had happened to me. I sat on the edge of the bed, resting my head in my hands, wishing to wake up from the painful and frightening nightmare. I finally got up, staggered towards the common bathroom at the end of the hall, and waited in line. My body ached all over. When it was my turn for the bathroom, I was shocked to see my torn and bloodstained dress, and noticed that my hair was sticky with blood and dog slobber. My nose was in a splint, my arm was in a sling, I had on a neck brace, and my front tooth was badly cracked. I removed the sling and the neck brace, but it didn't help my appearance. My eyes were swollen and already turning purple. Slowly, I began to remember bits and pieces of what had happened. A cold, numbing stillness crept over me. I winced, looking at the frightful face looking back at me in the mirror, and wondered, "Who am I?"

I left the building and walked aimlessly down the streets of Skid Row. I walked for hours. Presently, I passed the park where my grandpa and I spent time, but not even those memories gave me peace or comfort. It started getting dark. I continued to wander through the streets in trance-like state without direction.

I am not sure how, but I finally arrived at my neighbor's house, where I had left my kids. She abruptly opened the door. She was visibly up-set that I had left them with her longer than we had agreed, but she took one look at me, shock registering on her face, and suggested I call my social worker immediately. Instead, I gathered my kids and went home.

I was quickly overwhelmed; the kids were completely out of control. My oldest son headed to the refrigerator looking for food, the oth-er son played with the toilet by repeatedly flushing it, my daughter tugged on my dress and begged me to let her play next door, and my baby cried non-stop from colic. I felt a destructive, explosive rage building up within me. Startled by my frenzied state, the kids sensed something was wrong and began to cry. One by one and in haste, I began to fling them in the upstairs bedroom, my hands trembling. Fumbling with the room key, I finally locked them in and threw the key away to protect them from my mad, destructive rage. I ran out of the house to a neighborhood church to seek help, yelling and crying hysterically.

"Please, please! Somebody help me! Help me!"

A priest immediately approached and led me into a confessional. There was barely enough room to kneel and confess my sins to the priest behind the veiled screen. I was frantic. I cried, "Please help me, Father." I could not stay calm in the confessional. I did not know what to confess. I didn't know what to do. When he instructed me to repeat after him and began saying things I couldn't understand, I ran out of the confessional.

I ran towards the altar. My hysterical crying turned into anger when I looked up and saw the statue of Jesus hanging on the cross with blood all over his body. He looked emaciated and in pain. I stretched my arms out and yelled at him, *"Help me, Jesus! Please, if you can, help me!"* A thought interjected sharply into my mind. He could not help himself, how could he help me? Out of nowhere, two priests grabbed my arms, one on either side, and escorted me outside. I stumbled and fell on the front steps.

I sat in a daze at the bottom of the steps. I was in a state of shock and felt numb. I couldn't think. I returned home to call my social worker. It took so much effort to speak to them, requesting urgent help for my kids and me. Feeling drained, I curled in a fetal position on the living room floor facing the front entry door. What seemed far away, I could hear the kids crying upstairs, yelling, *"Mommy, open da door!"*

When my social worker and another woman walked into the house, they rushed upstairs. They forced the door open. "One by one, they took the kids" and walked them past me while I was still lying on the floor emotionless. And then a lady with my baby, Frank, in her arms passed me; I knew they were going to come back for me because how could they not rescue me, too. The door gently closed behind them. Slowly, I got up and looked out the window. In disbelief, I saw they were leaving! *"How could they leave me behind?"* I thought they were going to take all of us; a dwindling thought as hope began to fade. Looking out the window I became frantic in disbelief yelling and crying. *"Don't leave me! Im scared plessss! Take me"*

Just as the car was leaving, I could see my son, Paul, standing up in the back seat. He turned around and looked at me. Our eyes connected. "I could feel his reassurance, as if to say, *"Mom, it's going to be all right."* Then the blue government car drove away and they were gone.

I walked through the house, re-living the sounds of the kids playing hide and seek each complaining that one was picking on the other. "My heart deeply yearning for their presence and unconditional loving hugs." I began to feel disoriented trying figure out what happened and why? I passively noticed $20 and a business card that the social worker had left. I walked upstairs and entered the sparse furnished bedroom except for a few toys and sat on the cold, linoleum floor. My body began to shiver not from being cold but shock of the reality, my babies were taken away. The pain in my heart was immense eventually my tear dried-up. Consumed by grief and despair turned numb. I had no thought of suicide because I was already dead.

What seemed like hours sitting in the kid's bedroom, I forced myself to get up and walked to the kitchen and picked up the $20, as I proceeded to walk out from the house. I don't remember closing the door or looking back, even the memory of my baby's voices faded. My heart turned void and detached; an unfamiliar person without hope or direction consumed my being. I walked until the early hours of the morning, with nowhere to go and a crumbled twenty in my hand. Eventually I let it go and watched as it drifted away on a mild breeze.

"All suffering comes from separation from God"

God Positioning Spirit
Process of Discovery

Rebellion

Chapter Four: Decision

Awakened From Sleep

"Accepting responsibility for your reactions to events diminishes the blame you can place on others but also empowers you to change and move on." I realized years ago I could not love anyone until first loving myself, which gave me the freedom to validate and embrace my life experiences to change and move on"

- David N. Viscott, MD, Emotional Freedom

My long walk through the night led me to Agnews State Mental Hospital. I have no idea how I got there. I recognized it right away. I looked for the window where I had last seen my dad. Someone from the hospital greeted me and guided me into an office where eventually a man entered. He began talking to me and asking me questions. The more he spoke, the more I felt myself slipping away. I could see his mouth moving and hear his words, but couldn't make a connection.

They admitted me to the hospital. I was uncertain of the diagnosis, but it was obvious that I had checked out of one world and checked into another. During my intake, they had me sit in a large metal tub filled with water up to my neck, with water jets blasting disinfectant from all sides. A large-framed, expressionless, female nurse stood near the tub watching me. I didn't mind. I felt secure in my new world. I could just let go. There were others like me, locked in a catatonic state of darkness and silence. I became a compliant participant by adhering to the routines and strict instructions mandated by the serious, professor-looking doctors and the stern nurses with their clinking keys that echoed reminders of me being institutionalized.

Most days I would be in the common room sitting on a green vinyl armchair with a chrome armrest. I'd claimed it for myself as my safe haven in the midst of chaos. At night, I would sleep on a bed that was next to an iron-meshed window with protective wrought iron bars to prevent people from getting out. Sometimes the moonlight would shine in and distract me from the nightly chaotic sounds of more than 40 women with whom I shared a large dorm. One evening with my hands resting on my stomach, I felt a subtle movement inside, a feeling I knew all too well. In that moment, I felt my numb heart come alive with hope. I felt a desire to do something about my situation. Intuitively, I knew I had to keep my pregnancy a secret.

While in the common room, curled up in my favorite chair, I could hear this woman named Gail talking to somebody about how upset she was that her husband, who had committed her, seldom came to visit. She appeared fine to me. She had every reason to be angry with him. One day, I noticed Gail was sitting alone at a table near the nurse's station, which was regulated for anyone requesting paper and pencil. I was curious about what she was doing. I got up and sat next to her.

"I must get out!" she whispered to me. "You, too. Write a letter of release. You have a chance to get out of here. Do this now!"

She got a piece of paper and pencil and began writing. She instructed me to copy what she had written. I did not understand what she meant. I didn't want to be released! The thought terrified me. I copied it, neatly folded the paper and put it in my pocket.

One morning during activity supervision, I heard them call my name, Gail's name, and two other ladies' names. They told us to stand in line by the nurse's cage. A female nurse led the way while a male nurse trailed behind us. Without question, we followed them in an orderly fashion; it felt good to take a walk down the long, shiny corridor.

It did not matter that I did not know where I were going. Once we arrived at the medical section of the hospital, we were directed to sit on a bench. One at a time, the nurse took the two lady's before Gail and me into the therapy room; then one by one they were rolled out strapped to a gurney; they appeared to be asleep and whisked away down the long corridor. Gail became very agitated and resisted the two nurses who walked her into the room closing the door behind them. A nurse sat silently across from me, she reminded me of mom with the same expressionless look. What seemed forever the door opened as they wheeled Gail passed me, the three nurses shared a few words and to my surprise I was escorted me back to the common room, I had been spared from electric shock therapy.

The next time I saw Gail in the common room, she was different. She was submissive and withdrawn. Her animation was gone. What I saw jarred me. They had done something to her. I recalled her saying, "I must get out." I reached into my pocket and pulled out the folded paper she wrote for me to copy. Immediately, I requested that the nurse give me writing paper and a pencil and began writing my letter of release. It took much practice to copy Gail's letter. Periodically the patients and I were allowed to spend a short amount of time outside in the courtyard within the cyclone fence under close supervision.

One day I was leaning against the cold fence looking out onto the pathway when a nurse asked if I'd like to take a walk with her. She had gentle, deep brown eyes and brunette hair caught up in a bun. Her cap rested perfectly on her head. I nodded my head yes. With my arms still folded, I trotted along beside her down the pathway. We finally arrived at a two-story building labeled Building B. She unlocked the metal padded door. We entered a very large, high ceilinged room, surrounded by the same iron-meshed windows that reflected the sun onto the walls. The shiny, dark green and gray floor had smooth indentations throughout. The nurse instructed me to stay put, and that she would soon return.

It was eerie inside the large room. I stood in a corner near a large window waiting in amazement. I watched people wandering around the room without making eye contact, as if they were in a trance. Many were talking to themselves, making gestures as if someone was there listening to them. What really caught my attention was how they each managed to walk aimlessly without bumping into one another.

A Spark of Hope

A woman with long, gray, oily hair came into the room. She gestured at me to look at the imaginary baby in her arms. She had a proud, motherly expression with a slight smile for something I could not see. Through my imagination, I acknowledged her baby. That moment imprinted on my mind. I thought: *If I could imagine her baby, what if I could imagine my situation differently? Could I change the way I felt? Could I get rid of the emptiness I feel most of the time?* At that moment, the baby in my womb ignited a flame—a desire to learn something new and become different.

The nurse returned. The gray-haired frail lady still adoring her imaginary baby, disappeared in the maze of lost and forgotten souls. The nurse and I left the cold, creepy building. I was captivated by what I had learned from the gray-haired lady; her imaginary baby was as real to her as the baby in my womb was to me. Somehow, it made sense to me. As the nurse and I walked back to the courtyard, I picked up my pace to match hers, unfolded my arms, lifted up my head, and walked to her pace. To my surprise, I began to feel different, as if I was also a nurse. I felt a reassuring connection with her, as if I was going to be okay, as if I was somebody, too.

I don't know what actually happened in that moment, but in order to capture the same feeling I knew I would need to model myself after this particular nurse. She got a kick out of me walking like her; I truly believed it helped me find a new world of possibilities, much like the gray-haired lady who envisioned her baby, which obviously gave her love, purpose, and brought light into her darkness. I began to imagine myself as a nurse and modeled their every move. This gave me a sense of direction, purpose, and courage to write my letter of release. I found a whole, new world within me that I could control.

I began to imagine myself as a girl in a convent school, learning to be a nurse. There is no way in that place, on my own, that I could have thought of this creative way to help me find new meaning in life. It had to be this spiritual force (GPS) unknown to me at the time.

My mind was no longer foggy, but clear. I finally was given phone privileges. I wanted to take responsibility for my children, so my first step was to call my godmother, Espie, a successful restaurant owner who never had children. I explained my dilemma. I asked if she would care for my baby son, Frank, who was still in the shelter. Elated, she arranged with the social worker to pick him up.

The day finally arrived. I delivered a baby girl. Because I was in the system, I had no right to keep her. I couldn't even hold her; my baby's fate was to be in foster care. The nurse whisked her away and all I could see was a little bundle, wrapped securely, shielded from my eyes. My hospital stay was for seven days. I knew I had to do something quick. My first and only thought was to spare my precious baby girl from the shelter.

I contacted Espie again and asked if she could also take my baby daughter. While talking on the phone, I could hear Baby Frank cooing in the background. It was such a comforting sound. I was reassured that I had made the right decision for him. After a deep pause Espie agreed with three conditions. I had to agree to disassociate myself from my babies by never looking for them and never letting them know I was their mother, and give Espie the right to name my baby girl. I agreed. I immediately made the proper administrative arrangements to give full consent to Espie to take my baby.

That night I waited until the nurses' shift changed and snuck into the nursery. I picked up my baby daughter and held her. She was separated from the other babies because the hospital was going to move her to the shelter. When the nurses found me, they were infuriated; they had no choice but to let me hold and care for her through the remaining days I was in the hospital. I fed her, changed her diaper, and counted her toes and the hairs on her head. I enjoyed watching her stretch, yawning, as I soothed her back and scalp, running my fingers through her wispy, light colored, wavy hair. Her little hand grasped my index finger. It was as if we were holding onto each other, embracing every moment, until the morning came when I had to let her go.

"Your mind makes up your life, but only you can make up your mind."

A New Beginning

We were wheeled out to Espie, who was standing by her car in front of the hospital, beautifully dressed for the occasion. Excited, she held out her arms and I gave her my baby daughter. I noticed Baby Frank sitting in the back seat of Espie's car in the arms of his nanny. He looked healthy. Espie assured me my babies were in good hands and that they would have everything they needed. I felt comforted, knowing that for once I was doing something right for my babies. Espie, with my daughter in her arms, got into the car and motioned the driver to take off.

When they were gone, I was driven back to Agnews. During the drive, I had conflicting emotions, battling an internal war over my decision. Was I right or wrong to give up my baby? By the time we arrived at Agnews, I felt change was imminent and needed to put my situation in perspective and except that I had made the right decision and figure out what were my options to be discharged from the hospital. Though the thought was frightening I knew it was time.

Gail had given up. She was never the same after her electric shock therapy. She seldom spoke, which led me to believe her anger towards her husband had diminished. At least when she was angry with her husband she had something to talk about, but now she didn't even have that. Remembering her words, "I must get out," and how shocked I was upon seeing her after the electric shock therapy, was scary to say the least. One day at the mess hall while serving meals cafeteria style, I began to think the possibility of working as a server, once released from the hospital. That thought gave me hope to take the next step and write my letter. It took numerous attempts to write my release letter that was legible enough to submit. I knew that being a "walk-in" patient increased my chances of getting out, but the thought of being outside the walls terrified me. I did not know if I was fully ready to take responsibility for myself, but my yearning for my kids was greater than my fear of the unknown. I was ready to change my life.

While working on my letter, I sat for hours staring at the blank piece of paper. Finally, I decided to describe who I needed to be to take care of my children because they were the reason "why" I wanted to be released. I knew "what" I was going to do and "how" I was going to do it. However, I knew the person I was at that moment could not help me get out of the hospital. We had phone privileges so I called Mom and reached out to her. I informed her I was arranging to leave the hospital and asked if she would consider picking me up. To my surprise, she said yes. I had assumed I would not be welcomed into her home because she had a new life that consisted of a husband and two kids.

I sat in the phone booth; recoiling from feelings of hurt and shame, tears rolling down my cheeks. Mom had reminded me that I had no business being at Agnews. My favorite, kind nurse opened the slightly closed door, extended her hand, and assured me I had done the right thing. We walked back to the main room. I returned to the blank piece of paper, reflecting on my feelings from what Mom said about me being out of my mind for admitting myself into the hospital. I thought, well, if I was out of my mind, then why couldn't I put new things into my mind. Inspired by what I felt before when I was modeling myself after the nurse, I wrote down an imaginary version of myself. Even though this was not who I was now, I knew she was the person I needed to become in order to take responsibility for my life.

I looked around the room and one by one wrote down my observations of what the nurses were doing. On another piece of paper, I wrote out everything that people had said about me that I did not like, belittling words that hurt my feelings. As the list grew, my tears soaked the letter, smudging and wrinkling it to the point where it was almost unreadable. As I tried to read what I had written, my painful feelings diminished, and I began to laugh. I thought it was funny that I could not read my own tear-smudged letter. I started to laugh and began to feel better. By the end of the day my release request, or as I like to call it my "I am-letter" was filled with sentences that were ready to move me forward and away from the hospital. I sent in my letter and eventually I was discharged from Agnews. With a renewed sense of hope and spiritual enlightenment that allowed me to embrace and love myself, I felt whole, guided and secure with an assurance that everything was going to be all right.

"Decisions, not Conditions, Set the Course of Life"

Chapter Five: Determination

Seeking Identity

I was optimistic about my future. I definitely knew nursing was my field of interest. I had no idea how I was going to get there, but I knew that I had to keep focused in order to reach my goals. The day finally arrived for me to meet with the kid's pre-release social worker. She spent considerable time explaining a written one-year plan to help me get my kids out of foster care. A welfare worker helped me rent a small place, which was near my grandparent's house. The whole process was overwhelming. It took a week just to figure out the bus schedule to see the kids. I was given strict instructions not to have anyone stay a night or move in with me in jeopardy of losing custody.

One day my grandfather knocked at the door. It was cold outside. I invited Papa into the kitchen to keep warm and made him hot chocolate. He looked weathered and tired; I'm 70 years old, *"tengo 70 años"* he said, no one was hiring him to work the fields, that's all he knew, in a somber voice papa said; "what am I to do" *"que voy a hacer."* He sat quietly for hours. Before dark he asked if he could stay the night because Nana had been drinking and had kicked him out again. It tore my heart to have to say no to him. I sat next to him and said *"Mi papa Lo siento mucho, no puedo la trabajadora social me dijo que no."* (I'm so sorry, I can't the social worker told me no.) That I could not even have anyone stay the night. "I couldn't risk losing my kids again" I walked Papa to the door. We stepped into the freezing cold and hugged again with tears running down my face, he said "its ok my little girl, "be careful" *"está bien mehita, tenga cuidado."* The days were far in-between spending time with Papa. Not long after that night, he became very frail and sick within a year. Nana unable to care for him, admitted him to a convalescent hospital. I did visit him and, it was obvious he had given up, a feeling I knew very well; and within a month Papa died alone. When I received the news it was heartbreaking. Losing a loved one always seems to surface reflecting thoughts "what could I had done different?" I carried the pain of regret for a long time.

Life always has a way of testing our values. I dearly hold onto Papa's memory. He was the only person who treated me with love, and literally protected me from harm. He never asked for anything except for that one time. Many years later, again I found myself consumed with guilt for rejecting him. One night I was sitting on the bathroom floor crying missing him terribly. To my surprise I felt a sweet sense and presence. When I look up there was Papa; Looking Tall slender upright stature, he was wearing his favorite flannel shirt, khaki pants. I was surprised he was not wearing prescription eyeglasses or his sweat stained hat. Papa did not speak, yet his smile and glow assured me he had found eternal peace and happiness. From that moment I was instantly released from feeling guilty. I can't explain what happened or try to figure it out, but I know there is a heaven and I will be *"Con Mi Papa"* "with my papa" again and other loved ones.

My week consisted of going to my outpatient, psychiatric clinic appointments and visiting the kids in foster care. Sometimes I would visit my godmother's restaurant and wash dishes for extra money. It was an indirect connection to my babies because inside the restaurant was a huge picture of them. Soon, Espie asked that I not come back. I think she was concerned that her patrons would learn the truth about her kids or perhaps she was afraid I would take them back. Either way, I respected her request and did not return.

The year went by fast. In order to regain custody of my kids, I had to have a three-bedroom place to accommodate us all. A month before the day I was to pick up the kids, I found the perfect house. It was a few blocks near both public and private schools. I slowly fixed it up. I spent a lot of time hitting the garage sales and thrift stores, and my landlady, Mrs. Purshing, donated twin beds with mattresses for them. I finally got approval from my social worker.

The day finally came. I eagerly waited in front of my house. A blue county car parked in front. It was almost identical to the one that had taken my kids away. One by one, the social worker let my kids out of the car. They ran into my arms and we hugged tightly. Before I knew it, they dashed into the house and the back yard, happily running all over the place. As the social worker drove off in her blue car, I waved goodbye with my kids next to me. When she was gone, we entered our little home—together again.

The kids started public school right away, but I wanted them to attend a private school. Education had never been a priority in my family, so for me, it was important to provide it for my kids. After a year, I made an appointment with Principal Sister Ave Marie to see about enrolling the kids in Five Wounds, a private Catholic school and church. I had no money so I asked the sister if I could work for them, cleaning the rectory in exchange for tuition. Both Mother Superior and Sister Ava Marie agreed. Living a block away, I could walk the kids to school every day and work at the rectory. I also made extra money babysitting for a woman named Kim, but it was not enough. I decided to rent out one of the three bedrooms in my house and include meals. When Kim and her boyfriend, Ed, brought the baby over, I asked if they knew anyone who was looking to rent a room. They said they would think about it and left.

That night, after dinner, while the kids played with their toys in the living room, Kim and Ed came over to pick up Kim's baby. The smell of pot roast permeated our cozy, little house. After they left, I got the kids ready for bed. I bathed the boys first, put on their pajamas, and then bathed my precious, little Sandi, taking my time shampooing her hair. Her giggles made me laugh. Once all the kids were in their pajamas, they knelt by their beds and recited, "Now I lay me down to sleep, I pray the Lord to keep me safe, Amen." The boys, ages five and seven, slept together. Sandi, age six, had her own twin bed. I tucked them in, tenderly hugging the boys and smoothing Sandi's scalp and gently rubbing her back until she fell asleep. As I turned off the light,

I whispered, "Mommy loves you," and softly closed the door. By eight o'clock, they were asleep.

To my surprise, the doorbell rang. It was Ed, expressing interest in renting the room. I fixed up a plate of pot roast for him and listened as he talked about himself. He asked if I would also do his ironing for extra money. Within the hour, it was settled. Ed rented the spare bedroom near the laundry room, with meals and ironing included. He was 37, never married, without kids, and had completed military service, which to me translated into being a responsible, stable man. He immediately blended in and became a part of our family.

Now that my home felt stable and secure, I wanted to pursue becoming a nurse. Before I could do this, I had to resolve a couple physical issues. When Jack bucked his rifle into my mouth, he badly cracked my front tooth, which eventually decayed and created a hole between my front teeth. He had also yanked out fistfuls of hair from my scalp. While I was hospitalized, I developed two bald spots, one on each side of my head and on top. I was frail, but I had a steely determination to fulfill my goal of becoming a nurse. Whenever possible, I watched the soap opera, *General Hospital*, to keep me focused on my goal.

Every day I intently brushed my teeth and then several times a day stuffed the decayed hole with toilet paper. Money was tight. The kids wore uniforms to school so that helped keep costs down. I eventually bought a sewing machine and learned how to make simple summer clothes for the kids and me. My favorite store was the Salvation Army. One day I found the perfect black wig that matched what was left of my hair. I was never so happy. I could not wait to take it home and wash it. I finally felt normal.

My goal came to fruition the day I set foot on the campus of Campbell College (now West Valley College). I was afraid but excited at the same time. I made my way to the nursing department. I approached the receptionist, struggling to speak. My words finally surfaced through determination that overruled my fear. Awkwardly, I stammered out the words, "I . . . wa,na be . . . a . . . a nurse."

At the same time, I noticed an enclosed office window with the words "Dean of Nursing." I pointed to the window and stuttered, *"I . . . uh . . . wanna* see Mr. Dean." She hid a smile and said that the man in the office was the Dean of Nursing, not Mr. Dean. She got up, went to his office, asked if he was available, and with a look on her face that suggested she thought my request was funny led me to him. Feeling nervous, the only words that I could stammer out were, *"I wanta be, ah nurse ... what do.. I do?"*

The dean explained everything I needed to do to be admitted into Nursing. First, I had to pass college entrance exam and complete the prerequisites. Just listening to him, scribbling away making notes and trying to comprehend what he was saying, I faded in and out. I was in overload. I left his office, my head spinning, and went immediately to the bookstore to buy a dictionary to figure out what the heck the dean had said.

I was excited. I had a clear blueprint on how to reach my desired outcome. My schedule was frantic; I enjoyed taking the required courses: anatomy, chemistry and medical terminology. Despite everything I was feeling, I set my mind to it and kept the vision before me.

Over time, Ed and Kim broke up and he and I became a couple. He was not a romantic person, but as long as I cooked and ironed his clothes, he was content and we were happy. Then one morning I woke up with morning sickness. When I told Ed I was pregnant, he showed no emotion. The day I went into labor, he sent his brother-in-law to take me to the hospital where I gave birth to my precious daughter, Karyn.

The day finally arrived when I received my letter of acceptance into the Licensed Nursing program. There are no words to express how I felt, especially when wearing my nursing uniform on my first day of class. School was tough. I knew nothing about time management or how to study. Then, there were the kids. I always focused first on Karyn,with needed help from Sandi and Paul they made things easier. Danny helped with yard chores; he enjoyed being outside exploring. Ed worked long hours, arrived home to eat, and went to bed; I studied. The benefit of growing up with absent parents is that I was never told I couldn't do the impossible. I was exhausted, but loved every moment of my life.

On my 21st birthday, Ed tossed me a fifty-cent coin and suggested I celebrate at the local nightclub, saying, "Let's see how good you really are." Since he volunteered to watch the kids, I left without any hesitation. For the first time in my life, I entered a disco club. I was in awe, with loud music blasting, girls in birdcages dancing, and a mirrored ball hanging from the ceiling spinning sparkles around the room. It was obvious I had never been in a bar before. The bartender asked for my ID and brought me a tequila shooter, on the house, to celebrate my birthday. After that, I was in a daze. With all the attention I was getting, I felt special. I returned home, still dancing, laughing, and feeling proud and eager, to show Ed that I still had my fifty-cent coin. I was completely, stupid drunk. Ed met me at the door; he laughed and said, "You did good!"

Ed and I developed an acceptable relationship. It took time for me to realize that it was because he liked me. I learned that if a man said he loved me, I could expect pain to come with it. Being with Ed, I felt special that, in his own way, he loved me, even though he never said, "I love you." I felt assured that one day we would marry.

Right after Karyn's first birthday, I became pregnant again. I was nine months pregnant the day I received my nursing cap and pin, wobbling across the stage, with my kids, Ed, and my surprised mother looking on. I could not have planned my delivery any better. Ed took me to the hospital and I had my baby girl, Jojo—fast! It was as if she said, "Hurry up, Mom. Here I am. Let's get going." Fortunately, she was born during Spring break. I took a month off from school, to enjoy my little bundle of joy.

Shattered Dreams

Even though I studied, I fell behind in my classes. I needed help and a solution soon came when it was my turn to host the study group.

One of the students popped a small white pill and then passed one to another girl. She was glad the guy hadn't forgotten to bring what she said was the key to opening her mind to study. That was all I needed to hear. I popped a pill and within a short time my mind felt like I had consumed Webster's Dictionary. I had quick answers, and was like Donald Duck on steroids. We had fun studying and the time went by fast. After they left, I cleaned the house like a tornado.

The following week I bought ten more little white pills that arrived in a small baggie. The dealer suggested that I also buy downers, just in case I had trouble sleeping. He generously gave me a package deal. From then on, I was hooked, riding on a bad merry-go-round. I had trouble focusing on my studies and failed my mid-term exams.

The Nursing Department called me in. I already knew the verdict. I was dropped from the program. I had no one to blame but myself. I immediately packed up my nursing books and carried the heavy box to the basement. I sat half way down the stairs with the box on my lap, feeling sad to see my dream vanish because of my dumb decisions. I had hit a wall and lost sight of my vision.

I mentioned to a girlfriend that I desperately needed a job. She called her mom who was head of Human Resources at a major hospital. She set up an appointment for me. They hired me on the spot, with full medical and dental. I found a dependable babysitter and within a week I was on the day shift for three months, and then went to swing shift after that, with extra pay. It was a great job, but I did not realize the consequence of being away from the kids, working the 3 to 11 evening shift.

For those three months, I was stress free. I enjoyed dancing to the sounds of loud music with Baby Jojo strapped to my chest. The kids and I played hide and seek, the boys would outrun each other to hide under the bed giggling. I'd run after them with my hands extended, shouting, "I'm gonna get you, tickle, tickle." Shrieks fo laughter filled the house and little Karyn, barely walking, would toddle after me, squealing, "Mommy, mommy, me get you," with her little fingers trying to tickle me.

During this time, Ed would hang out with us after dinner to watch television instead of going straight to sleep. With five kids in our little house, we decided it was time to buy a house to accommodate our expanded family. I enjoyed making our new home beautiful and hung my Harriet apron in the kitchen to anchor the thought that I had finally arrived at fulfilling my childhood dream. I was ecstatic. It had happened so fast.

When I took the job, I hadn't given much thought to how long it would take for me to drive to work or to drop off Karyn and Jojo at day-care, with every minute counting to get to work by seven. I had to depend on the older kids to get themselves ready for school. Ed pretty much kept to himself. We ate dinner together, but he found it difficult to talk to me. Most of time, he would ask one of the kids to tell me what he needed, even if I was in the room. After dinner, he would sit in his favorite chair and fall asleep. Karyn and Jojo would climb up onto his lap and cuddle on his rolling belly, falling asleep to the sound of his snoring. The boys entertained themselves before bedtime while Sandi and I had our girl time together. I enjoyed brushing her beautiful long hair.

As a family, we would go to the Monterey coast to spend the weekend. As the designated driver, I took the scenic route along the Carmel coastline so I could see the estate homes and golf courses lining the Pacific Ocean. It was breathtaking. The people who owned these estates intrigued me. I wondered what they believed about themselves that helped them achieve such an amazing lifestyle. Did living in those huge homes make them happy, or did being happy attract the homes to them? Was that lifestyle a burden or was it taken for granted? I seldom saw the owners, but it was obvious the groundskeepers enjoyed the fruits of their labor. After we reached our destination, we would rent a motel room with a swimming pool. The kids and I would walk on the beach, collecting seashells, and our day would end watching the sunset, eating sandwiches. We treasured these experiences.

At the time, Ed and I lived in the east foothills of San Jose. I enjoyed exploring well-established, developed communities near downtown.

As I drove around, I would tell the kids that one day we would live where the streets were lined with maple trees, where they could play in the streets, walk to school, have a library nearby and parks with swings. Then there it was . . . the neighborhood of my dreams! It looked like a movie set, where kids played kick ball in their front yards, with beautiful custom homes on both side, and maple trees perfectly lining the street. I frequently visited the courthouse down-town and walked straight to the basement where real estate probate listings hung openly on a clip board. In disbelief there it was, the house on Maple Street. Within a week Ed and I with a realtor entered the home. A son of the deceased elderly couple walked through our dream home.

I loved Ed and accepted his ways. Old habits are hard to break Ed raised in a home with five over protective sisters and doting moth-er. He was accustomed to having his own way. Surprisingly, nothing much had changed since he rented the room from me. He paid for room and board and bought grocery, when he got home from work, he expected the house to be clean and his clothes washed and ironed. Beyond that, he didn't expect much. I learned to keep my distance when he came home late because it meant he had been drinking after work. I seldom took his verbal abuse personally because it was his personality, just more so when he drank.

I believed his drinking was due to the uncertainty of our living ar-rangement. I knew our relationship would change for the better once we got married. I mustered up the courage to bring the subject to his attention. I did not know what to expect.

"Ed, do you want to marry me?"

"No," he said, quickly and insensitively, mumbling something under his breath. I thought he was playing with me. I couldn't believe he would say no like that.

"WHAT!"

"NO!" he shouted without hesitation. "Didn't you hear me? What the hell is wrong with you? I said, NO!"

"Why not?" I cried. "What's wrong with me?" He ignored me, walked away, and went to bed. I was stunned. His response pierced my heart and opened a floodgate of emotions that came from all the abuse in my past.

I ran to the bathroom, looking for something to take the pain away. There was nothing there. Sobbing, I looked in the mirror at my stricken face, wondering what in the hell was wrong with me, covering my mouth so the kids wouldn't hear me cry. I entered the bedroom. Ed was already snoring. I searched the drawers for "downers," hoping I might find one hidden amongst my past. When that failed, I went into the kitchen and found Ed's bottle of booze above the kitchen cupboard. I poured a large drink of whiskey and sat outside in the back porch, drinking and sobbing.

From that moment on, I began to detach emotionally from Ed. Other than that, nothing much changed. The kids loved Ed. They were happy. I was not. I knew I needed to figure out what the HELL was wrong with me! Why wouldn't he want to marry me? I needed to find my identity—whatever that was, and I still needed to keep stability for the kids, which Ed symbolized and provided.

I yearned for Ed's attention because I wanted his love. It was soon apparent that he had created a world that did not include me, only my kids. Again, I felt undesirable, unloved, without identity or direction. I tried to capture the part of me that had hope, imagination, and unstoppable momentum, the "me" who loved to dance, and believed in capturing the dream that turned into a nightmare. There I was again recycling my past, the only difference this time, I picked-up where Ed and the others had left off, I became the abuser to myself emotionally inflicting pain to a wounded soul.

"Michelangelo carved out of marble the beauty hidden within the rock"

Chapter Six: Denial

The Devil's Grip

I spent less and less quality time with my kids. My working swing shifts, with only every third weekend off, didn't allow us much time to be together. Ed had full responsibility of the kids, even though they were very self-sufficient. At the hospital after my shift, I would change my uniform to street clothes and stop at a local bar for a few drinks before my long drive home. I knew that as long as I arrived home before three in the morning, Ed would not lock me out of the house. This habit became the highlight of my day.

For years, I would cash my payroll check at a bank near the hospital. One day as I approached the bank, I noticed a security guard escorting a man out of the bank. Unsympathetically, I thought, "Fool." I took a double take. It was Frank, the heroin addict, who I had not seen since I was 16 years old. I walked over to him. Surprisingly, Frank remembered me and said my name. I took him back into the bank and cashed his personal check. We hugged our goodbyes and I thanked him for sparing my life. He looked at me as if he didn't know what I was talking about, but it did not matter. With money now in his hand, he hurriedly walked away to shoot up the evil venom and drift away into the abyss of darkness.

As he staggered down the street, I sat in my car, keeping an eye on him until he eventually disappeared. A deep sadness overwhelmed me, remembering the 16-year-old girl who was so desperate to find her place in life, and who was just as lost now. I thought about that night when I begged Frank and extended my arm for a shot of heroin. I remembered his words, "No. God has plans for you." Anger welled up inside me. *God! God who?*

In a sullen mood, I drove to the bar for a few drinks and to listen to the other regulars tell their usual stories, filled with an undercurrent of sadness and regret. I appeased my conscience with thinking, what else mattered? When I arrived, Johnny, the bartender, already had my usual drink on the bar. I sarcastically made a toast to the 16-year-old part of me. I raised my drink and said, "This is for you, dummy girl! One day we will be free and find happiness!" After two more drinks, I left and headed home.

The next morning, I spontaneously woke up thinking of Dad with a strong sense to find him, which was a strange thought; I had ruled Dad out of my life and had no interest to see him again. I hadn't thought about him but coincidentally, while updating personal information in the college administrative office, a pleasant lady at the front desk began to help me fill out necessary forms, when she realized I was her niece, my dad's sister. I was somewhat surprised as I had not seen her since I was six. She was openly friendly and eagerly talked about my Dad to a deaf ear. She told me that he lived within 25 miles of my house with his family of over 20 years. And now several years later there I was, trying to remember what she had said about where Dad lived. I recalled that she mentioned he lived behind a well-known grocery store. At least I remembered that much.

I drove to his neighborhood, parked my car behind the grocery store, and slowly walked up the street (no doubt, being guided by GPS) and mid-block I came to a small wood house. I opened a gate and walked down a garden pathway, noticing the garden had not been watered for some time. A lady saw me through the window, opened the door, and called my name. She welcomed me into the house and introduced herself as Maria, Dad's wife of 20 years. She led me into a very small room where my Dad lay, swollen and yellow. He was surprised and happy to see me, as was I. My original desire was to get answers as to why he had left me, and to tell him how his leaving without explanation had affected my life. That was no longer important.

Maria helped me get him up from the bed. We gently walked him outside to sit in a chair in the backyard. I sat on the grass with my head in his lap, his hand resting on my head. We sat silently, basking in the warm sun. No words were needed. Our moment of reconciliation magically erased all the unanswered questions. All that mattered was being together again.

After a while, Dad got tired and we got him back into bed. I applied alcohol to his chest, arms, and forehead to keep his frail body cool. It was soon time for me to leave. I kissed him on the forehead and promised to return in the morning. It felt so freeing and healing. As I stood in the living room saying my goodbyes, I noticed numerous family pictures on the wall of Dad's beautiful family: they all looked happy. I got in my car and drove off, feeling restored and amazed at our time together.

As promised and with equal urgency, I drove back to Dad's house the next morning. I immediately noticed the fence gate was open. I knocked on the door. To my surprise, no one answered. I walked in and went straight into Dad's bedroom. It was empty. I called Maria's name, but she didn't answer. I ran out and drove to the nearest hospital. I double-parked and rushed to the front desk, inquiring if my dad had been admitted during the night. The front desk clerk directed me to the fourth floor.

I was eager to see Dad again, to hold him in my arms, and talk about my life and how much I loved him. As I entered the room, I stopped in shock. There he was—all alone, lying on a gurney, with a sheet covering his face. I pulled back the sheet to see him, thinking about how Dad's life had ended. My heart filled with sadness. Tears streamed from my eyes. I was comforted to know that Dad had found happiness with his new family. As I covered his face with the sheet, I felt a supernatural presence near me. I was in awe of all that had transpired within the last 24 hours. *What if I hadn't intuitively obeyed the sense of urgency the day before to find Dad? What if I had never found him and missed the opportunity to heal and restore our troubled hearts?* It was unthinkable. My mind was still seeking answers; especially, what had awakened me with that sense of urgency to see him when I had not wanted to see him for so many years? *Who or what had guided me to find Dad, to be with him in his last hours on earth?*

After a life of heavy drinking, cirrhosis of the liver became his K.O that ended his life. While embracing the experience of being with Dad, I was sad that he had come to his end at a time when I was trying to find my beginning. The following week, I attended Dad's funeral and met my brothers and sisters. Leaving the cemetery, I said goodbye to my newfound siblings.

In my mind, I could hear Dad hollering at ringside, "Get up! Get up! Don't let that f___ knock you down!" I thought, about those years Dad fighting to live his dream, when all along, his decision to drink alcohol became his silent opponent that took his life.

I embraced my memories of Dad; good or not, he was still my Daddy. I stopped drinking for a while, as a tribute to Dad. Seeing him yellow-skinned, in pain and miserable, I was scared enough to stop. I knew I did not have a problem drinking like Dad or my grandparents, or even a problem popping diet pills like Mom. I had it all under control!

"Death of a loved Awakens Destiny. A Cause for Action!

Hope at My Door

One afternoon, while washing dishes and looking out the window admiring the beautiful maple tree turning color in the early fall, I saw my two youngest girls, Jojo and Karyn, walking eagerly towards the house with a new neighborhood friend. I gasped as they drew closer. As they entered the door, still in stunned disbelief, I waited to welcome their friend, who they excitedly introduced to me as Hope—my own baby girl. I thought, "What an appropriate name."

Hope had curly, light brown hair, big brown eyes, and an exuberant smile. She looked healthy and happy. I told Hope that I knew her mom. She smiled. I reached out and gave her a welcoming hug, breathing in the fragrance of her hair. It was the first time since she was a day old that I was able to hold her. The girls, still giggling, pleaded with me, "Please, Mom, can Hope spend the night?"

Still stunned, I savored the moment, feeling my heart flutter with joy as the yearning for my baby girl was fulfilled. I knew how upset her mom, Espie, would become, once she found out Hope's newfound friends were actually her sisters. I handed Hope the phone to call her mom to let her know she had arrived from school safe, and was at her friends' house, and wanted to spend the night. Then she handed me the phone to talk to Espie. When Espie realized it was I, she was upset and questioned if I had anything to do with the girls meeting each other. I told her I was shocked by their chance meeting and ventured to say that my girls wanted Hope to stay the night. Surprisingly, she agreed.

I understood her shock. I was also thinking, what were the odds of this happening? Hearing Espie's voice triggered the memory of the last time we had met. It was at her lawyer's office to sign the papers for her legal guardianship of my two children and my agreement that I would not attempt to see Frank or Hope. She had shown me pictures of the kids who were of pre-school age. It was obvious she loved them very much. At that time, Espie had expressed an interest in adopting the kids. She said she would contact me to sign the papers. She also mentioned that if at any time we crossed paths, I would be introduced as a distant aunt. It had been years since our lawyer visit. Espie never contacted me to sign adoption papers and I had never pursued her request.

Now, here was Hope, ten years old, and in my house. That night when it was time to tuck the girls into bed, I asked Hope if I could tuck her in like I did Jojo and Karyn. She said yes. I ran my fingers through her curly hair, gently soothing her scalp and back until she fell asleep. That moment was more precious than anything I could imagine. I took her home the next day. When the nanny opened the door, I caught a glimpse of my son, Frank, playing in the backyard.

Courage Begins with an Inward Battle

Ed loved his routine of going to work and coming home to the kids. We never discussed marriage again. Even though there was never any romance between us, it would have been nice to be friends, but we seldom spoke. In order to function in our living situation and not feel emotionally deprived, I focused on my personal growth. I left the hospital and registered at a junior college. I enrolled in the only class available, which was Sales & Marketing. At orientation, I realized that the marketing class was not a shopping course. The class was way over my head.

At the break, the professor saw I was leaving and asked me to stay. He said he would help me. I stayed. Within a year, I competed in leadership debates, which helped me to resolve my issues about not being heard. I participated in many speaking opportunities. Along with other students, I was awarded a trip to the University of Mexico City. I felt unstoppable and craved the challenge to express myself.

Periodically, I still visited my favorite bar to meet up with the regulars and catch up on their life stories. I looked forward to seeing Johnny, the bartender, who was funny and always had something good to say. I learned that he knew my brother from the past (whatever that meant). I liked talking to Johnny. Whatever I talked about, he listened. Making a connection was important to me. I hungered for it. One night the bar was empty, and our usual conversation shifted into something more serious. I asked him a series of questions, one being that if he had a wish, what would he do differently and what prevented him from achieving his goals? He laughed and said he wished he had someone like me who was ambitious to help him fulfill his dream of starting a commercial painting company. That must have been how he knew my brother because Robert had become a house painter after his release from prison, years earlier.

I asked him specifically what would his life be like if he wasn't a bar-tender. To my surprise, he asked me what my goals in life were and why. I told him I wanted to marry a man with mutual interests like camping and riding motorcycles. I wanted a married social life that involved consistent family outings. I also wanted to buy a house in the same community Ed and I lived in, but I wanted to give the kids the option of living with Ed or me. In my mind, I had it all figured out. I wrote everything down; how our life together would material-ize. As I left the bar, Johnny shouted, "let's do it!" On my way home, I was convinced that Johnny was my ticket out. For once, I had clear direction, purpose, and a commitment to take the challenge. For once, I would know "who in the hell" I was.

Several weeks passed without my saying anything. I wanted to talk to Ed about my plans, but kept changing my mind because there was no use discussing anything with him. It was frustrating to live with someone who would not communicate. Our friendship had ended. I had to do something. I had decided to marry Johnny because I need-ed more variety in my life. Johnny said he needed a woman like me to help him reach his goals in life, so by marrying him I would have a purpose. I did not consider the kids' views in my selfish quest for marriage because I knew as teenagers; they would probably want to live with Ed, their dad, anyway.

"GPS Insight - In the realm of uncertainty, purpose of life is found"

Johnny and I got married. We did not have a wedding or anything special because our marriage was more of a business arrangement. We signed a contract that we would annul the marriage within a year. The moment I said, "I do," I was heartbroken and wanted to go home to Ed and the kids. I knew what I had done was morally wrong and immediately regretted my decision. The uncertainty I faced with Johnny scared me, but at the same time, I was excited. There was no turning back. I had found my way out. I was determined to do more things that were fun with the kids besides driving and sightseeing, while Ed slept.

It's amazing how those two words, "I do," can change everything, especially when you're missing the main ingredient: love. I did not understand the value of marriage, and eventually grew resentful. Nothing had really changed, except now my life was split in two because several times a week I would go to Ed's to clean the house and fix dinner for him and the kids.

I had a year's "to do" list, but within six months everything was done. Johnny's commercial painting company surprisingly became a quick success. He hired my brother, but I didn't like them hanging out at the house together because I knew Robert was still using hard drugs. Johnny and I bought a home in the same beautiful community, only a few streets from the kids and their school. We bought a bunch of toys, like a camper and two Kawasaki dirt bikes. The weekends were fun, but not enough to overcome my uneasiness and guilt feelings regarding the mess I had made. I had no way out of the pain I felt for what I had done to my family, especially to Ed. I knew I needed to make things right.

Over the next few months, I realized Johnny and Robert were dealing drugs. I was horrified to find that the painting business was just a front. Johnny's behavior changed drastically and it was obvious he was consuming more drugs then he was selling. He was extremely jealous and abusive and his moods were uncontrollable and unpredictable. I sent the kids to stay with their dad, Ed.

Eventually, I was fed up with Johnny, particularly when he was stoned on drugs. I actually played on his temper, daring him to fight just to see him stumble around. Many times in my rage, I would pick up anything within reach and fling it towards him. What was scary was that I was becoming more destructive than Johnny without the excuse of being loaded. The situation got so bad; I moved out of the house, accepted my losses and filed for annulment.

It came time for me to leave San Jose and live on my own, San Diego was my destination. Early on in our marriage, Johnny and I had taken a trip to Calexico to visit his mother and passed through San

Diego. I knew one day I would live there. I cleaned motel rooms, while applying for work at various hospitals. I became stable enough to attend interior design school, which I enjoyed immensely. However, Johnny found me and pleaded with me to give him a second chance.

"I love you. Trust me. I promise I won't hurt you," he begged. "(*Hm, no memory recall*).

Regrettably, I gave in. Within a short time, his old behavior resurfaced. My life was again unstable. Fortunately, a major hospital hired me and I rented a house for my kids and me. Then the unthinkable happened. Within the month, Johnny and my brother followed me and moved into a house across the street. By that time, I was afraid of Johnny. He was unpredictable and abusive. I tried to diffuse his irrational behavior and to stop him from stalking me, but I couldn't. My life became unbearable. My oldest son began having disciplinary problems, and I was powerless to help him. I knew his behavior was a cry for help, a warning for me to wake up from my own self-destructive lifestyle that was damaging my children's lives.

Finally, I returned to Ed's house. The kids were happy again and soon settled back into their old life. I was deflated and disgusted with myself. I became a loner; my only companion was Jack Daniels, and on weekends, I took amphetamines in an attempt to control my emotions. All the while, I was trying to get my life back on track. I applied for a labor delivery nurse position at a hospital in San Francisco. When I was hired, I was ecstatic. Even though the commute was long, I didn't mind. I entertained myself with a pint of whiskey, listening to Oldies music while enjoying the ride.

One night at work, we had several deliveries and were short staffed. I enjoyed the rush. Every delivery was an amazing experience. Receiving newborn babies directly from the delivery doctor to prepare for the mother's arms was amazing and an awesome responsibility. Most dads chose to be in the delivery room, although after several hours of being verbally abused by their wives during peak labor, they were emotionally exhausted. Once instructed to "gown up," they got their second wind, cheering on their wives, for the final payoff, the big push to the finish line and tears of happiness, celebrating a home run with their newborn held in their arms.

That evening driving home, I began to reflect on how the moms looked being wheeled in, all prettied up for the long-awaited grand debut, then during their stages of labor, all their vanity and poise vanish. They cry for help, begging and pleading, to minimize the pain, screaming for an epidural, "hurry up!" to numb the excruciatingly painful contraction. When I explained to them how pain helps contract the uterus to position "their precious gift" to be born, something quickened within me. It was like an epiphany. I was receiving a revelation. I desired to be reborn. It was a strange realization. I shrugged it off, numbing my pain with JD - Jack Daniels, my epidural.

Finally, arriving at the city limits with the empty bottle beside me, I began to feel sick to my stomach and light-headed. I was ready to pass out. It was about three in morning. I stopped at a car dealership parking lot to throw up. I lurched out of the car and sprawled face down on the winter frost grass. It felt good. I passed out for a short spell, the car still running and the music playing. I woke up and got back into the car. I was a mess. I was scared, but eventually made it home. I sat outside my house, covered in vomit, waiting until five in the morning when Ed would open the door.

While waiting, I thought about the crazy things I had done while drinking. Once I had found a commercial margarita blender in the back seat of the car and couldn't remember how it got there. Another time, when it was pitch dark I went down to the base of the Golden Gate Bridge to hear the sound of the turbulent water. Staggering about in dense fog on my climb back up to the car, I slipped and grabbed a shrub, narrowly escaping a watery death. I remembered racing my car at three in the morning. I was going over a hundred miles an hour for several miles on a major expressway. I wanted to see how many red lights I could miss. With one DUI arrest on my record, it was only a matter of time before I hit the point of no return like my Dad, or worse, hurting or causing a fatality of another human being.

My drinking, much like my life, was out of control. Betrayal is painful, especially by a loved one, but it is devastating when you betray yourself. I had made a promise to myself that I would never become like Mom or Dad. Needless to say, it was a self-fulfilling prophecy. "Never say Never".

Time with Mom

I would periodically visit Mom, who I loved very much. She appeared to have a wonderful life. She adored her two sons and showered them with affection. She was a dutiful wife and appeared to be happy. My sister, Silvia, who got along with Mom and her new husband, would go out to dance clubs with them. Mom still enjoyed dressing up. She looked beautiful as ever with her blonde wig, her favorite lipstick and robust body.

Ever since I could remember, Mom struggled with her weight. She always took diet and water pills in hopes of getting thin. When she was diagnosed with diabetes, she went downhill. She neglected herself and eventually stopped wearing her blonde wig and lipstick. She wrapped her hair with a scarf and became a recluse, only caring for her boys and husband. On one of my unexpected visits, I found Mom sitting in a dark living room, arms crossed. She was not suicidal, but something was wrong. She asked me to take her to the emergency room.

While speaking to the doctor, she began crying. Seeing my mom cry stunned me. My heart filled with pain for her. I had never seen her cry before. The doctor gave her anti-depressants. We left the emergency room, and nothing was ever spoken about that day. I was concerned about her taking anti-depressants, along with the sleeping pills, diet pills, and diabetic medication, but at least she had stopped drinking.

One day Mom called me unexpectedly. She asked me to take her to a lady who would pray to heal her legs. I had never heard of such a thing. I hesitated, but complied with my mom's request. We arrived at the lady's house. Mom had difficulty walking up the stairs to the front door. The lady introduced herself as Carmen. She invited us in. I decided to wait in the car. I was spooked to see her living room walls covered with pictures of Jesus Christ, and he was not on a cross. An hour later, Mom easily walked down the stairs with Carmen behind her.

Mom got into the car without help and Carmen came to my window, indicating she needed to talk to me. She noticed my hesitation, and then said it was very important that we talk. I left Mom in the car and followed her, still thinking how sad it was for Mom to resort to this craziness. I felt very uneasy.

As we sat down in the small room, Carmen opened up in prayer and said God had spoken to her. I became rude. I stood up halfway and asked if she was a psychic. She looked straight into my eyes and said with convincing clarity, "No, it's time for you to realize that God is calling you. You will receive confirmation when seven things happen. You have free will to choose." She started speaking with what sounded like a foreign language, but every word resonated within my heart. None of what she was saying made any sense to me:

1. *Overshadowed by darkness*

2. *The sound of construction near water without kids*

3. *Spiritual Battle*

4. *The lady welcomes*

5. *Insight revelation*

6. *Healing transformation*

7. *Help the Children*

By the time she was finished, my whole body was perspiring and shaking. She asked me for permission to pray. Although her prayer was beautiful, I could not wait to get out of there. I never believed in that stuff, but I couldn't forget what Carmen said.

In the Devil's Grip

One night, a year later, as the kids were sleeping in their rooms and I could hear Ed in his bedroom snoring, I got comfortable on the living room sofa and fell into a deep sleep. Suddenly, I felt a heavy presence in the room, hovering above me, and I woke up. There was a dark, evil presence pulsating above my body. Startled, I tried to open my eyes. This overbearing presence was on top of me. I attempted to move, squirming, moaning, unable to yell for help, my body paralyzed with fear. I was finally able to open my eyes and saw a huge, dark grayish cloud-like presence. Its form was part man and part animal, hovering above me with glaring eyes. I was terrified. One minute I was looking at myself on the sofa, moaning in the grip of this entity, and the next I was back in my body.

Finally breaking free, I fell off the sofa and crawled to the bedroom, shaking in terror. I got into bed with Ed, pleading with him to hold me. In his usual sarcastic way, he asked if I had been drinking. I cried, "No! I'm not drinking! No! Hold Me. Hold Me!" As I lay trembling, Ed held me securely in his big burly arms. As soon as he did, Carmen's first words, "overshadowed by darkness," came to my mind. *Was this real? What did it all mean? Overshadowed by darkness.* I was filled with fear, questions, and confusion. I had not been drinking or taking drugs for a long time, for at least several months. I concluded that my long work hours and long commute were messing with my mind, so I rented a furnished room near the hospital to make my life easier.

A few months later, one early morning when I was at my apartment, my sleep was interrupted by the sounds of construction. Immediately I again thought about what Carmen had said and could hear her saying, "the sound of construction near water without kids." It was number two on her list. Realizing I was also near water, alone without my kids, I raced home to make sure they were okay. *"The sound of construction near water without kids"*. On my way home, I bought a small Bible, stopped at a Catholic church, sprinkled holy water on me and my new Bible, got on my knees, and prayed.

Soon afterwards, a distant friend introduced me to her cousin, Steve, and we set up a date to meet at a nightclub in San Jose. On my way there, I took a short cut through a residential area to catch the freeway. My car quit working unexpectedly. It was not out of gas. It just wouldn't start. I noticed a small building with several cars parked out front. I entered and asked a lady if I could use the phone. She signaled me to follow her upstairs. She motioned to me to sit down. She didn't appear to hear a word I said. I looked over the balcony, and then it hit me; I was in a church.

The lights dimmed, and a man, standing behind a podium, said, "God is calling you!" Two men approached him and they fell gracefully unto the blue carpet. Heat filled my body. I broke out into a sweat. I headed down the steps thinking, "I'm out of here," but instead found myself drawn to the front, walking towards him and into an amazing, seamless, ultra-bright, white light—and remembered no more.

Time passed. I heard the sound of a vacuum cleaner in the distance. My eyes opened and I saw that I was covered by drapes from head to toe. The place was empty, except for an elderly lady who had apparently covered my legs with drapes and was waiting for me to wake up. I propped myself onto my elbows. She gently helped me get up. No words were exchanged. I walked to the empty parking lot and got into my car. It started without any problem.

I drove on to the nightclub and Steve was still there waiting for me and asked, what had happened. I guess I looked the way I felt; different. All I wanted to do was go home to be with my family. We said our good-byes and agreed to meet up again soon.

A few weeks passed and I was still feeling displaced. Fortunately, it was my long weekend off so I had four days to reflect on what had happened. The day I returned to work I found out I was scheduled for the outpatient clinic. I was to assist that morning with an abortion procedure. Afterwards, while sterilizing the equipment with a pressurized water hose, the suction tube became clogged. I increased the pressure. I held the end of the tube in one hand and applied water pressure with the other, when an intact lifeless fetus flushed out unto my gloved hand. I was horrified. The fetus fit perfectly in the palm of my hand. I tenderly touched its head, hands and knees, tears running down my face. I was deeply affected by my part in the procedure that had ended this precious life. My heart awakened with compassion. It was a new feeling for me. Something had shifted within me. I managed to finish my shift and the following day I gave my notice and resigned.

I kept remembering, seeing, and feeling the fetus in the palm of my hand and each time felt extremely sad. Several weeks had passed since I had resigned from the hospital. I needed some much-needed R&R. I decided to check out the place where my car had broken down. I drove back the following Sunday and saw that it was a non-denominational church. I was clueless as to what that meant. The greeters were friendly, yet I felt embarrassed, hoping I wouldn't run across the drape lady.

I decided to sit in front, three rows back, to see if there was a gimmick to explain the ultra-bright, white light I had seen. The music started and a huge choir dressed in blue gowns entered from behind the podium. The singing was amazing, beautiful and uplifting. The director made a motion with his hands and the 100-member choir sat down in unison. I was very impressed. A man began speaking about the church's activities. I grew bored and wanted to leave. I looked around for an escape and in full view of me, was Carmen sitting next to the elderly lady who had stopped me on my way to Jack's house, so long ago, who said God wanted me. I was literally shaken to my core; quivering as her words resonated through my mind, "God wants you!"

With tears running down my face, I felt deep remorse. The devil had a strong grip on me. I realized I was in *a spiritual battle*. I was faced with my past, present and future. Who would win? That pivotal moment was my moment of decision.

God Positioning Spirit
Process of Discovery

Rebirth

Chapter Seven: Displaced

GPS (God Positioning Spirit) Makes a House Call

I started dating Steve, the cousin of my distant friend from San Francisco. I really liked him. When I mentioned about my baffling church experience, he listened and even mentioned an interest in attending the church with me one day. I thought it would be nice to check it out again with him. He also invited me to New York for the weekend. It was very grand. We went first class, drinking, laughing, and having a good time. As we approached New York, the pilot's voice came over the intercom to look out the left side window. As I saw the Statue of Liberty below me, the pilot announced, "The lady welcomes you." I put my drink down, completely sober. *The lady welcomes*. It was the fourth message on Carmen's list. Three more and supposedly I would have to choose.

For now, life was good. Steve captured my heart and soon proposed to me. We headed to Nevada to get married. This time was different because we were in love. We rented a house on the other side of town. My whole focus was now on my husband. My kids moved back and forth between Ed and me.

We joined a church and I got involved in the choir. Everything was perfect. We fit in. I had a husband that I loved. I looked like what I believed a Christian woman should look like. I cut my long hair short, began wearing longer skirts and applied minimal makeup, if at all. I even attended the church socials. I liked it that Steve was more than eager to attend fellowship with me after church and he eventually joined the choir. Steve became Mr. Social. He loved the attention and I loved to see him happy. He was emphatic about meeting up with the same group of friends for coffee. He even made it a point to have social Fridays. I didn't go with him because I liked spending more time with the kids, especially being around Sandi who was now in high school. One Tuesday night at choir practice, I "heard" or intuitively "felt" something" (GPS) point out a 28-year-old girl, and I "knew" she was having an affair with my husband. I realized it was Carmen's fifth prophecy: *Insight Revelation*. I quickly dismissed it and thought to myself, "Don't mess this one up. He loves you."

Later, I attended a seminar at a Holiday Inn, which ended at ten p.m. As I was getting into my car, I saw Steve and the girl leaving the hotel together. I confronted them. He said they were having "fellowship" at the coffee shop inside the hotel and the others had already left. I desperately wanted to believe him. He began to spend more time with her while I spent more time at church, praying for wisdom and understanding. Heartbroken, I could not understand how these things could happen in a church. I thought it must be because I was not a good wife. I was lacking something essential; otherwise, Steve wouldn't need this girl's friendship. We had several heated discussions about her, which always ended with him telling me to leave him alone and to stop nagging him.

On one of those occasions, I gave him back my wedding ring and moved across the street into a small apartment with my youngest daughter, Jojo. With the exception of Monday "church was closed" I continued to go to church, which became the only place I felt safe. One evening when the choir was being televised, the choir director put me in the front row next to Steve's "friend", Andréa. Before the camera began rolling, I noticed she was wearing my wedding ring. I gasped and said, *"Hay, that's my ring!"* She replied with an attitude *"Well, it's mine now."* The camera started rolling; we were signaled to stand up and begin to sing and praised God together. Tears running down my face I felt so much love for God; with a deep sense of trust and assurance. To surrender the pain and admit that this was bigger than I could handle alone.

Later, the choir director called me into the office and said he knew of the issues between Steve and me. He asked *me* to resign from the choir. Shocked and angry, I did as he requested but continued to attend the church. My husband and his girlfriend continued their relationship, but eventually dropped out of the choir and then the church.

I had difficulty giving up on Steve and our marriage. I became obsessed with him, much as Johnny, the stalker, had become with me. One day Steve called and asked me to come over to his house. I was hoping he wanted to make our marriage work. Instead, he told me he was not cut out for marriage and as he enjoyed his relationship with Andrea and wanted to continue it, he wanted a divorce. I pleaded with him to make things work, not to leave me. He was unmoved and escorted me out of his house.

For weeks, I felt conflicting, raw emotions, thinking something was definitely wrong with me. Things like this don't happen in church! Steve infidelity made me feel spiteful, angry and vindictive towards men, and yet, I still had an inexplicable compassion for them.

Almost a year passed before I finally recovered from my break-up with Steve. I found a job working for a non-profit organization to help men and women transition through re-training from incarceration to employment. My specific position was to work with ex-cons, recently released from prison, and help them re-enter the world. I served as their counselor and life coach, teaching them skills to change how they felt and believed about themselves. We had much in common. We had freedom, but we were still locked in our past, in our regrets. I found it interesting that the very thing I was teaching became lessons learned from my own life.

The uncertainty and turbulence of my life started to rub off on my kids. Even though they were respectful kids, as teenagers they started to act out. Being away from home so much, I was not keeping track of what they were doing. I felt responsible for their actions because of my bad choices.

One night, my daughter Karyn did not return home from school. Fearing she had been abducted, I called the police to file a missing person's report. What was heart breaking was that the police officer, who was filling out the report, knew more about Karyn than I did. He knew she had become involved in a gang. He informed me that unless she had committed a crime, she was not a priority. Days turned into months, and I was worried sick, wondering where Karyn was, tormented by fear for her safety.

I was determined to find her. Every night I drove to the gang hot spots on the east side of San Jose, asking around for Karyn in hopes of finding her and bringing her home. Ed threatened me, saying that if anything happened to her, I would not live to see the next day. Ed's threats were justified. I accepted full responsibility. I knew it was my fault that Karyn had run away from home. Had I been a stay-at-home mom, a better mom, Karyn would not have run away.

Even though my heart was breaking over Karyn, I enjoyed my job and every day looked forward to going to work. I knew I had much to learn and was determined to listen more from them and ask questions about their lives as children. I had the privilege of talking to Jessie, an ex-gang member who changed the course of his life. We spent time talking about gang life from his perspective. He helped me understand that Karyn had chosen to get involved in gang life because she was getting from them what she was not getting at home—a family. He also clued me in on a critical point; Karyn most likely had changed her name. Listening to Jessie gave me a glimpse into the reality of gang life.

Early one morning Jessie did not show up for our usual meeting. He was later found down the street from my office, dead, murdered execution style. That was gang life. I was saddened when I heard the news. Jessie had been very optimistic about his life. He had started working. He had just become engaged. He once told me that for the first time since being a kid, he was happy. "It's never too late," he had said. Those words rang deep in my head.

From that point forward, I became involved in the Gang Task Force in hopes of finding my daughter. I learned that many heart-broken mothers were losing their children to gang life at an epidemic rate. It shook me up. I could not change my past or the ripple effects it had on my family, but I knew that if I continued to live in my past, it would poison not only me, but also my family—like snake venom without an antidote. I knew I could help those who cried out for help, but I had to obtain the resources and had much to learn. I was passionate about making a difference helping this targeted group of kids and at the same time, I believed I would someday, find Karyn. Somehow, I trusted that I was on the right track, moving forward. At the same time making a difference helping parents in similar situation to develop a support group program at their church, school and community.

- What I expected from relationships became clues to what I needed to do for myself first.

- First clue of dysfunction was my children's behavior; and how they reflected my disposition and unhealthy life decisions.

"The day our memories become larger than our dreams is the day our soul begins to shrink"
–Ike Reighard

One by one, my kids succumbed to a dysfunctional lifestyle, with the exception of my youngest daughter, Jojo. She spent more time with her dad, Ed, the stable pillar of the family. The house felt empty. It was painful to see the kids attempting to move upward in life but falling far short. I had nothing to offer them, not even hope for things to change.

One day I was walking to work in downtown San Jose, waiting for the traffic light to turn green when I noticed a car turning right. I recognized the driver. It was Espie. She looked just as surprised to see me as our paths crossed again. She indicated that she needed to talk to me, but the cars behind her honked for her to move. I did not pursue her afterwards. She had not appeared frantic, so I assumed that my children, Hope and Frank, were all right.

My primary focus was on my job. My boss, Kenneth, was a compassionate and creative man who was committed to serving his community. As a teenager, he had been involved in gangs and was driven to find solutions to the growing epidemic affecting young people. Under his tutelage, I was growing and the program was growing. I was reassigned to work specifically with women in transition from prison. That change became a major turning point in my life. Their pain reflected my own imprisoned heart.

Several months later, a lady called, informing me that Espie had passed away. My first reaction was to rush to see Hope and Frank and finally tell them the truth about who I was, but then I thought that maybe it was better to keep it a secret. I wondered why the lady had called me. No one was supposed to know about me. As far as I knew, only Espie knew. Who else knew? My children deserved to know the truth. If I didn't tell them, I feared someone else might.

I arrived quickly at the house. A woman, who I suspected might be one of Espie's relatives, opened the door to me. She certainly didn't look grief-stricken. She led me into the living room without questioning who I was. It was odd. She called Hope in from the bedroom and told her I had something to tell her, and then she left. I was shocked and unsure about my approach, since it was obvious that this insensitive woman wanted me to tell Hope the truth. My daughter walked in looking despondent and sad. As soon as she saw me, she called me "Auntie" and ran to me. I held her in my arms, and then gently sat her down next to me on the sofa.

She lifted her chin and looked deep into my soul. Somehow, I knew that she knew what I was going to say. I was speechless. Our souls were still engaged when my son, Ron, who was now sixteen, walked into the room. I got up and hugged him. They sat down together, expectantly, waiting for my over-due message. It was a surreal moment for the three of us. I knew what I had to say would add to their grief.

I was as gentle as I could possibly be and to the point. I gave them the short version of what had happened, why Espie had raised them as her own children. I told them that ultimately it was because two women had loved them dearly. I apologized and asked them to forgive me. I expressed my love for them, and said again that they had two moms who loved them very much.

Frank immediately left the room without saying anything. I did not follow him because he appeared to be okay with my revelation. Hope led me silently to the front door. It was time for me to leave. In our silence, no words were necessary. I wanted to take them with me, but I trusted that Espie had left them financially secure, as promised. I left my address and contact information.

I was confused, questioning if I had done the right thing while hating myself for not following through with Espie's request to meet earlier. I returned to an empty house that matched my own heart, mind, and soul. I kept feeling the kids' grief and pain as sharp as if it were my own. I questioned my decision; their pain was beyond comprehension. Why did I have to shatter the only life they had known? Just reflecting on my kid's faces was so painful. I wanted to return and hold them close. However, this was their private time to grieve for their mom—the mom who had raised them and maybe even for the mom who had given them away.

I went to the medicine cabinet where I kept my drugs. I opened the door, but then closed it. I felt disoriented, grieved to the heart. I opened the door, and then closed it again. I began pacing the house, going from room to room, desperately trying to capture the good memories of my family, only to realize how my poor choices had damaged the lives of my children, each struggling to find their own place in life. Their lack of direction had resulted in them taking drugs, drinking, prison, abuse, and betrayal, and my precious Karyn—recruited into a gang. I didn't know if she was alive or dead. One by one, I saw my kids' faces flash into my mind like a video on replay. Their suffering was tearing my heart wide open. It was more than I could handle.

I began pacing and talking to myself, crying hysterically. I was in emotional labor, attempting to purge inner demons that were tearing me apart. I yelled at myself. I vilified my nature. I was like a diseased, insane leopard seeking revenge. I started thinking of the people who had said, "God wants you" and "God loves you."

In deep, remorseful pain, with hot tears streaming from my eyes, mucus dripping from my nose and slobber spilling from my mouth, I cried, tore at my skin and pulled my hair, literally beating myself with self-hatred and vengeance. My body poured sweat from the intensity of my rage. I reached a point in my anguish that I looked up and shook my fists toward Heaven.

"God, you messed up! If you exist, you made a mistake! I am a mistake! God, help my kids! Please spare them!"

Unable to stop crying, anguished hysteria rising up from the core of my being, I cried out, "God, who are you? I can't take this pain anymore. My heart hurts too much."

I swung my arms around, remembering the abuse, the rejection, and the oppression that the little innocent girl within me had suffered.

"Why God? Why does it have to hurt so much?"

The little girl in me, as if crying for her parent's affection and love, was now crying out for a miracle to ease her emotional pain and torment. With the last breath I had in me, I reached out to God.

"Whoever you are, help me. My pain is too much. Please, God, help me! I can't anymore! God, "Take the Pain Away!"

Suddenly, from my core came a rupture of immense bluish, luminous light, much like the light I'd seen at the church. It filled the room, whirling and swirling around me, wrapping about me like a cocoon, wrapping me in pure love. While in its embrace, it laid me gently on the carpet. My tears of despair turned into a warm, secure, divine-filled peace.

After a while, I opened my eyes and jumped up, questioning what had just happened. With my hands clenched into fists, extended upward, I cried out.

"DON'T MESS WITH ME GOD! I can't take it anymore!"

From every fiber of my being, in a surrendering hope, I cried, *"God, help me! Father God, Daddy, HELP ME!"*

Still crying, again the amazing light filled the whole room, swirling all around and covering me just like a blanket around a newborn baby, gently laying me back onto the carpet. A sweet, comforting, bold, loving, holy presence (which I now know as God Positioning Spirit) said, *Awaken, my children. Your children will be restored.* My whole body pulsed with pure love. In a state of loving assurance and fulfillment, I fell into a deep, restful sleep.

The following morning, I opened my eyes, stretched out my arms and legs, and looked around. Everything looked brighter, including the ugly, brown carpet where I lay. All my emotional turmoil had disappeared. I felt re-born. Without a doubt, I had a *healing transformation*, the sixth item in Carmen's revelation, leaving the seventh to be fulfilled.

Like an infant learning to crawl, I rolled onto my knees and took my time getting up. I slowly walked to the bathroom, looked in the mirror, and rather than seeing a depleted, toxic woman, I looked and felt different. My face was bright and clear. I was alert and rested. I knew peace for the first time, the fear and tension inside was gone, and my body vibrated with love. I opened the medicine cabinet and one by one emptied each bottle that had controlled my life, flushing the pills down the toilet.

In that pivotal moment, on May 11, 1979, at 4:20 p.m., God Positioning Spirit (GPS) made a house call.

The following day, after my encounter with God, I was sitting in the living room, reflecting on my experience with awe. After a while, I heard the same bold, loving voice from within instructing me to drive to Story Road and McLaughlin Avenue. It made no logical sense, but without hesitation, I got in my car and drove to that destination. At the corner of those two streets, to my utter amazement, standing near a bus stop bench, leaning on a sign pole, was Karyn, my long-lost daughter.

Elated to see her, I got out of the car and as soon as I walked towards her, I heard GPS say, "Tell her God loves her, and then let her go, get in the car, and leave." It was obvious that street life had taken its toll on my 15-year-old baby girl. She looked world-weary. She had black hair, shaved brows, black lipstick, wore black clothes, and had tattoos. Our eyes connected. I saw and felt her pain. We both cried, amazed to see each other again. In a tired, sad voice, Karyn said, *"Mom, take me home."* Releasing her, I gently raised her chin, looked into her eyes, and said, *"God loves you, Karyn, and I love you so much."* Then I let her go and walked back to the car. I heard her crying out, *"Mom, take me home!"*

While driving away, I looked in the rear view mirror and saw her head slump down as she leaned back against the light pole. The moment was so surreal. I felt guided and knew I was doing the right thing. I finally arrived home, still savoring Karyn's hug, and amazed that I had the strength to leave her. The next Sunday, a girl knocked on my door and asked my name. I responded and she signaled towards a car. To my surprise, Karyn got out and ran towards me, crying, "Mommy, I love you. I want to come home. I need help. Do you really think God loves me?"

"God is more interested in changing us than changing our circumstances"

Awakened World Within

My children and friends asked what had happened to me because my demeanor had drastically changed. I was no longer the life of the party (or the happy drunk) because I was at peace. Everything changed after my experience with GPS, or the Holy Spirit, which I knew was preparing me for change.

Several months later, my boss called a mandatory staff meeting to announce that my position had been terminated. I initially felt a wave of hurt, but intuitively believed there was something greater waiting for me. I had to move out of my house. Feeling uncharacteristically optimistic and at peace, I began packing up the house. In the process, I came across a business card from the vice president of a well-known life insurance company, who I had met while I was in college at the National Leadership Marketing competition. He had suggested then that I consider the insurance profession. To my surprise, when I called him, he remembered me and scheduled an appointment for me to meet with the vice president of the Northern California branch.

Before long, I was hired, given an advance, and rented a smaller house on the east side of town. The kids were on their own, attempting to redirect their lives. Sandi, Paul and Frank entered trade school and became self-sufficient. Danny married and moved away. Hope kept to herself, living with her aunt. Karyn found the love of her life and was happy. It was just Jojo and I, living in our little house.

I was given six months to pass the state exam, which was a grueling experience. I took the exam but failed, missing it by two points. I was given another opportunity to take the test again before the six-month deadline. In the meantime, I landed a million dollar business account with a welding company and earned a huge commission.

In a casual conversation, one of my client asked me about my long-term goal in the insurance business. I mentioned the exam ahead of me and we laughed because it was obvious I was not looking forward to taking the test again. He said, "The reason I'm asking is that our southern branch office sure could use a sales person like you." I pondered the thought: live in Orange County? How perfect!

"Set me up," I said. He immediately picked up the phone. Within the week, I flew into Burbank Airport for an interview, and I was hired on the spot. I was given a two-week advance to move to Orange County. As soon as I returned home, I invited my kids to a barbecue, and announced that I was moving to Orange County with their sister, Jojo. From that day on, everything fell into place. I bought a one-way, Greyhound bus ticket and gave almost everything I owned to Sandi for her home and sold the rest.

Before Jojo and I moved to Orange County, a friend of mine introduced me to her acquaintance, Josie, who lived in Santa Ana. She agreed to pick us up at the Greyhound Station in Los Angeles. After a ten-hour bus ride, Jojo and I happily arrived. I had no idea the bus station was so huge. People were everywhere, scrambling in and out of busses. We sat ourselves down on our two large cardboard boxes, packed with our essentials, and waited for Josie. I began to question my decision, realizing that I did not even have her phone number.

Out of nowhere, I heard in the distance someone calling my name. The place was so noisy I stood up, looking around, and seeing no one. Jojo and I looked at each other and shrugged. Again, we heard my name. It was Josie. Sweeping us into a welcoming hug, she was equally happy to meet us. She took us to Alvarado Street for dinner. It was filled with gaiety, vibrant colors, vendors, and restaurants with music playing. My mind filled with fond, childhood memories of *Salsi Puedes* and the people who sang while they worked in the open fields. After a long drive to her house, Jojo and I welcomed the tiny twin bed where we snuggled together and fell asleep.

Within a few days, my new job at a waste management company provided me with a car and an advance to rent a place. Within two weeks, I found a small apartment located on Peace Street in a cul-de-sac. The neighbors were very friendly and Jo immediately found a girlfriend whose parents allowed her to stay with them when I ran late getting home from work. My next and final task on my list was to enroll Jo into a private school.

It was a week before Labor Day, and the administration office was open. A lady asked Jo's name to find her application. I told her she was not pre-registered. The lady looked at me with a sweet, sympathetic smile as my daughter sat quietly, looking embarrassed. She took out a tablet with a long list of names on a waiting list. She wrote Jo's name at the bottom and apologized. I put my hand out to stop what she was saying, and peacefully told her that God had directed me to this school and that Jo was to begin now. The lady asked for my contact number and indicated the school would get back to me. The following week I received a call and Jo and I met with the dean of the school. Within an hour, she was accepted and enrolled in the high school.

Everything fell into place. With a good salary, plus commission, a car with a Thomas Guide and GPS, there was no way I could get lost. There was nothing to divert me. One day at the office, my boss, Leo, gave me an invitation to attend a major client's annual Christmas party at a five-star hotel in Los Angeles. I had absolutely no interest, but Leo insisted that I go. The day arrived and I was still hesitant. I did not own a holiday outfit; all I had was my favorite simple cream-colored dress, so I bought a red flower to look somewhat in season. I reluctantly drove to the grand hotel, which was beaming richly with Christmas lights.

While waiting for the valet, conscious of my low status, I unconsciously detached from GPS and reverted to my past behavior patterns. Negative thoughts about how dumb and stupid I was consumed my mind. *What's a woman with seven kids and a messed up past doing at a place like this?* I was beaten before I even entered the hotel. I was an emotional mess by the time I entered the hotel lobby.

What was worse was that the hotel foyer was breathtaking, filled with beautifully decorated Christmas trees. There was live music in the air. Lavishly dressed, "beautiful" people were walking around with drinks in their hands, talking, laughing, and singing Christmas carols in harmony with the band. I had no idea which direction to take. My first inclination was to find the powder room. As I walked toward it, I noticed the huge Oak Room, reserved for the company party I was to attend. It was already packed with what appeared to be mostly couples. My stomach clenched, and I made a beeline to the bathroom and locked myself in a toilet stall, feeling very self-conscious.

I felt so out of place, my mind was scrambling. I remembered my favorite television soap opera, *All My Children*, and decided to pretend to be Erica Kane, Susan Lucci's character. She would blend perfectly into this social event. I began to imitate her, feeling the surge of confidence as I left the powder room and entered the private dining room. I sat down at the first open seat next to a gentleman. Still nervous, I had forgotten to ask if the chair was taken. I self-consciously stood up, but he kindly said, "No, please sit down."

Before I knew it, the salad was served. Not having mastered the use of multiple forks, I paused, looking confused. The man, whose name was Angelo, noticed my hesitancy and made a joke about it. We both laughed and the next thing I knew, dinner was over. It was perfect. He liked talking and his diverse knowledge kept me intrigued. Before I left, he offered to introduce me to potential clients in the waste management industry.

Weeks later, Angelo called and invited me to lunch at an elegant private restaurant on Rodeo Drive. I was rather surprised not to see anyone else meeting us. During lunch, he noticed I was uneasy. He pulled out a list of contacts for me. He had already set up times for me to see them. After that, I relaxed enough to enjoy his unpretentious demeanor. He loved to talk about world history. I was like a kid, absorbing his every word. I was impressed with his knowledge. I thought he must be old to know all this stuff. I could not help myself; I had to ask! He was Ed's age, a month older, but a completely different kind of person. The lunch crowd was gone, except for two people, huddled in conversation on the other side of the room. It felt very intimate. I quickly said goodbye, and left, saying I wanted to avoid the traffic heading home.

While driving home, my mind replayed our conversation, especially when I asked him about his family. He mentioned that he had a wife, Rosie, but no children. He said she had been ill but was progressing well and ended that conversation. I was trying to make sense of our luncheon and understand what I was feeling. Perhaps I had over-played Erica's role. From that point forward, I decided I would not meet with him except for business purposes and only at a public place.

A month passed and I periodically caught myself thinking about him. It was refreshing to be with him. I felt amazingly comfortable with him. At work, I was building up a good client base. Leo was pleased. During our weekly sales meeting, he suggested that I explore connecting with people involved in building casinos in Palm Springs. I promised to look into it, but felt it was way out of my league and only focused on small industrial companies in the area. One day, Vince, my immediate supervisor, invited me to attend a casino's grand opening in Palm Springs.

I had never been to Palm Springs. The parking lot at the casino was like a car show. There were Maserati's, Rolls Royce's and a line of Mercedes Benzes. Vince and I came in the back way so that he could measure the truck ramp for a trash compactor. His intent was to prepare a proposal just in case someone on the sales team made a contact. I was helping him take measurements when a beautiful, deep burgundy Rolls Royce passed us and parked near the back entrance. To my surprise, Angelo got out and walked up to us. I introduced Vince to Angelo, who then invited us to the grand opening celebration. I felt pretty special. Angelo took the time to introduce us to his partners.

On the ride home, Vince talked about nothing else, ecstatic over the commission on the potential deal. He went on and on, and all I thought about was how special Angelo made me feel, personally introducing me to politicians, builders, and of course, his business partners and lawyers. In Vince's excitement, he had even forgotten to complete the measurements for the trash compactor.

When Leo heard about our successful venture, he was adamant that I pursue the contact. Vince did not like that and neither did I. Leo didn't let up, constantly reminding me that there was only a small window of time to present a bid. To my surprise, Angelo called me first and asked to meet at a local coffee shop. I eagerly accepted. It had been seven months since we had first met. It felt like our paths had crossed on purpose, and now that we were finally reunited, he had reached a secret place in my heart. Deeply confused, I asked GPS, *When was the last time I spent consumed by your sweet fragrance?*

I heard a faint response. *If you have to try to recall, then it's been some time.*

However, at that moment, I became pre-occupied with Angelo and felt a love connection. At that moment, I betrayed my first love and values and re-entered the seductive world of illusion. Angelo held my hand and said, "I want you to quit your job so that we can spend more time together. You will not have to worry about a thing." He assured me that one day, we would get married. Those words ran deep, fulfilling an aching desire to hear those words and feel that kind of love. I opened the door to the secret place in my heart to him and said yes.

Angelo quickly arranged for Jojo and I to move closer to his house. Although I was ecstatic and seemingly happy, in that instant, I felt a deep mourning in my soul. It was indescribable. My conscience wouldn't leave me alone. My love for Angelo overruled everything. I knew what I was doing was wrong. I just couldn't change it. Unknowingly, my mourning turned into anger and I became spiteful. He was good to me, but all wrong for me.

No wrong goes unnoticed. Our burdens reflect and attract like kind. As I sought to recapture a first love, I compromised my values and betrayed GPS, totally convincing myself that I could bite the apple without consequences.

Conscious Conviction

My son, Paul, the family confidant and catalyst, called me with the news that my son, Frank, was in jail. I flew to San Jose to visit him. It was heartbreaking to see him, in his early 20s, incarcerated. He had committed a terrible crime, pled guilty and accepted responsibility for his actions. I recalled that as a child, he was diagnosed as hyperactive and put on Ritalin. Through most of his early school years, he had been bullied. One time a kid threw a rock at him, hitting him in the eye, impairing his vision. It was obvious that his hard life had deeply bruised his soul.

He was sentenced to 25 years without chance of early release. I couldn't bear to see him behind bars, dressed in an orange jumpsuit, looking so helpless. No words can express the pain and guilt I felt looking at my son.

Life continues to remind us of the consequences of our actions and the far-reaching effects of our poor decisions. As we sat facing each other, with plate glass keeping us apart, I knew that I had made the right decision telling him I was his biological mother. If I had not, he would have thought himself all alone. I could not change his past, but I could redirect the course of his life by changing mine. Love heals. It brings light into dark places. I knew my son's terrible fate, but I also believed in love, prayers, faith and trust in God's promises. What the devil intended to destroy, God would use for good.

The External World Reflects Our Decisions

After my visit with Frank concluded, I went to visit my mom. I knocked on the door. No one responded. I walked in. I found her lying in bed, in the dark, helpless. I asked what was wrong and she began to cry. Her husband was having an affair with her friend. I was at a loss for words.

How could I comfort her, knowing I was guilty of being the other woman in my own illegitimate relationship with Angelo? Hearing Mom's words of pain and betrayal, I was faced with the reality that I was doing the same thing to Angelo's wife, Rosie. I gave Mom a hug, and encouraged her to get up and get dinner ready for her family. Filled with sudden shame, I couldn't get out of there any faster. I sat in the car, trembling, thinking about how Mom had finally achieved a beautiful home life, but had failed to keep the man she loved from her closest friend. I knew she would be all right, but I had absolutely no words of comfort to give her.

That same year, Mom had a stroke. Jojo and I drove all day to San Jose to be with her. I had much I wanted to say to her, but because I was not in a good place, I did not know how. When we got to the hospital, it was difficult to see her in that condition. A nurse entered the room and placed a food tray near her bed. She left, assuming I would feed her. I did my best, but just as I got the food to her mouth, Mom snapped her mouth shut. It struck me like a slap how selfish she was. All the old stored up feelings of rejection, anger, and betrayal as a child rose to the surface. My hand quivered as I tried to almost force-feed her. I was shocked by my own reaction.

I realized that Mom and I were much alike. We both desired love and connection and had failed miserably because of our unhealthy decisions. We were two adult women, driven by passion, who had made major mistakes with the men we loved. We had come full circle together. Here was an opportunity to heal our unresolved past. All that mattered was to love Mom and be present with her. Then she made a mess in her underwear. With love and forgiveness now in my heart, I felt anger dissipate as I cleaned her up. I felt real empathy for Mom for the first time in my life. The little girl inside me finally was able to touch, help, and love her mom without fear of being pushed away. The doctor assured us that Mom's life was not in danger. She would recover.

While still in San Jose, I kept thinking of my daughter, Hope. Years had passed and I had no idea where she was. When I had visited Frank in jail, he mentioned that his sister was living safely with a family somewhere on 17th Street. Before I returned home to Orange County, I drove around the area, looking for her. As I drove on 16th street, I saw a girl walking by. I pulled up. It was Hope! I parked, walked toward her and intersected her path. In disbelief, we looked into each other's eyes and our souls united as we embraced. Another GPS experience had come to fruition.

God never ceases to amaze me. Even though I had felt disconnected, He still guided me through the darkened streets to find the light of my life, my baby girl, Hope. We spent time catching up. She was now a mature woman and had coped well with the loss of her mother, Espie. She shared that she had a boyfriend and was hopeful about her life. I gave her my address, drove her home, and met with the family who was taking care of her. I asked her to consider staying with me before making her final decision about her boyfriend, but when I thought of home, I realized I was living a lie. I felt great shame about my deceptive life. I knew I needed to first trust GPS to guide me through the obstacle course ahead of me and to have faith. GPS would make my way straight.

How soon one forgets lessons learned, only to re-do the very thing we promise ourselves never to do again. The good thing is that emotions are like internal messengers, reminding us to seek healthier solutions. We find ourselves doing the very thing we dislike in others, which reflects a similarity in ourselves, our "painful reminders."

While having a quiet time with Mom in the hospital, I began to think about the women in my family—Nana, mom, my sister, me. A common thread wove through our lives—the need to be loved and to feel significant. My grandmother died alone, Mom was betrayed, and I was living a shameful lie. In my mind's eye, I thought of each of my children. Just a few years earlier, they knew God had restored me. I knew what I needed to do differently to redirect my life and pave the way for the future generations. I was responsible for my children. Life was no longer about me. I needed to act on the promise of God. I knew GPS was waiting for my decision to do the right thing. Carmen's seventh point, *Help the Children,* had to be fulfilled.

"Preoccupying thoughts pave the way, therefore your journey"

Chapter Eight: Direction

Power of Decision

With my mind now, set on what I had to do, I returned home to Orange County to meet with Angelo. I met him for coffee the following day. He could see immediately that something was wrong. I started right off by openly talking about my emptiness. Seeing how Mom was a victim of infidelity and in pain as a result, my heart opened and I felt convicted because I was committing adultery. I could no longer endure the pain. All he said was, "Yes, I know something has to change." He offered no solution, so I knew I had to end our relationship. I was tired of living a double-standard life. I asked him if Rosie's health had improved. He passively said, "Yes, slightly," but his body language said, "Why are you going there?" He stood up and said, "Everything will turn out fine," and left. He did not understand that everything was not fine. I was dying inside my soul. I was heartbroken from the pain I had caused. This was something Angelo could not fix.

That afternoon, I decided to pay a visit to Rosie at her home, located in an upscale estate community on the hill. I felt guided by GPS and felt assured of what I was doing when I walked up to the door. I knocked. Rosie opened the door and invited me in. She apparently knew who I was and guided me upstairs to her master bedroom suite. Being in their bedroom was like rubbing salt in my wound, but I felt she was justified. In a numbed state, with tears in my eyes, I poured out my heart, kneeled before her, and asked for her forgiveness. As she sat stoically on her bed, she told me she had known about our relationship all along (as well as the other women in her husband's life), and knew his relationship with me was different. We didn't say much after that. After a while, Rosie escorted me to the door. I spent the remainder of the day waiting for the consequences of my decision.

It wasn't until the next day that Angelo came over. Normally he would knock on the door before coming in, but this time he entered without knocking. Without any words of explanation—only his furious expression conveying *what the hell have you done?*—he threw $575.00 at me and informed me that he and Rosie were going on a two-week vacation. He wanted me out of his house before they came back and to leave the keys behind.

After he left, I was completely stunned. I knew he would not forgive me for what I had done and that there was no turning back, which was what I had wanted. He made the decision and although it was very painful, I knew it had to be done. As soon as the door slammed behind him, my heart grieved terribly, yearning for him. I felt drained and hopeless, crying from a broken heart.

I lit a candle, sat in my favorite chair in the bedroom, and focused on the little flicker of light that began to brighten the darkness in the room. It reminded me that God never leaves us, even in the darkest of times. Once again, I had consciously derailed my life. I sat in the dark, silently praying, and was inspired to read Isaiah 43, verse 19: *For I am about to do something new. See, I have already begun! Do you not see it? I will make a pathway through the wilderness. I will create rivers in the dry wasteland.*

I was drained, exhausted from crying. I fell into a deep sleep. When I awoke, the morning sun was shining on my face. The candle had burned down to the silver protective plate. I felt consciously clear in my mind and heart. I made a pot of coffee, brought in the newspaper, and began the task to find a new place to live. I was thankful that Jojo was visiting her dad because I had much to accomplish in two weeks. I called several rental ads without any success because they required either credit verification, large deposits, or didn't allow children. The first two days were discouraging. I felt overwhelmed.

One day while I was at the grocery store buying a newspaper, I also picked up the weekly Penny Saver. When I got home, I browsed it for rentals. On one page a picture of a beautiful home for sale captured my attention. I sighed, knowing the house of my dreams was way out of reach, and then returned to the section on rentals. I searched for rooms, apartments, and houses without any luck. The days were passing and my time was running out. I accumulated stacks of news-papers and Penny Savers. After a week, I picked up another Penny Saver and saw the same ad for the ranch-style house. Written in bold print, the house was listed at $135,000. It had three bedrooms, two bathrooms, two fireplaces, and a custom built swimming pool with a waterfall. I sighed, put it away, and continued making phone calls. Each time I was rejected because I did not have a job, credit cards, a bank account, or references, plus I only had $575 in my hand. It was getting late. I was restless. I needed to get out of the house and take a drive.

On a lark, I retrieved the address of the ranch-style house and within 30 minutes, I was parked in front of it. A large moving van was in the driveway. A man, removing the Open House sign, noticed me sitting in the car. He waved for me to enter. His wife walked me through the house, showing me its features. It was even more stunning than the picture in the paper.

"Well, what do you think of it," the man asked me.

"*It's beautiful*. It's the perfect place for Jojo and me. It has everything I ever dreamed about having."

It was late, and I could see that the man and his wife were tired. I prepared to leave. He asked, "Will you promise to come back tomor-row?"

I promised, even though I knew there was no chance for me to buy their house.

That night I could not sleep. My mind kept going to the house, think-ing about what colors I would use to decorate it. The following morning, I continued the regimen of calling on rental ads. Even though I was frantic about finding a place to rent, my mind was on that beautiful house the entire day. I wanted to keep my promise to the couple, so I drove back to their house. I apologized for being late. The truck in the driveway was completely loaded. The couple appeared to be happy to see me. They introduced themselves as the Spencer's as we sat at the kitchen table. Mr. Spencer asked if I was ready to make an offer on the house. Without thinking, I said, "Yes, I love the home." They both replied, "We can see that. We know this home is yours" and asked for my offer.

I offered all I had, $500. Then I told them that I didn't have a bank account, credit cards, or references. Mr. and Mrs. Spencer looked at me intently and said, "Sold." I couldn't believe my ears. Mr. Spencer added, "The moving truck is packed, but by any chance do you need any furniture?" Everything the Spencer's mentioned, I needed. Right then and there, they drew up the papers, took my $500, and we signed an agreement. The Spencer's informed me that a mortgage company would finalize the purchase and contact me.

Mrs. Spencer walked me through the house, showing me how to use the kitchen's built-in appliances, the greenhouse, swimming pool with the waterfall switch, and much more. It turned out that Mr. Spencer had custom-built the house and that he and his wife had raised their children there and were ready to move on. Mr. Spencer handed me a folder with the house's 20-year history, including blueprints. The house was in perfect condition. The truck driver closed the doors and the Spencer's handed me all of the keys and left.

I stood on the front porch, keys in my hand, waving goodbye to them, stunned at what had happened. My heart was pounding. I was filled with joy and peace knowing GPS had blessed me again. This moment reminded me of the scripture Proverbs 3, verse 21: *My child, don't lose sight of common sense and discernment; hang on to them.*

The pool lights were on and I dipped my feet in the water. Little ripples formed and expanded until they reached the other side of the pool. I sensed God Positioning Spirit telling me that a little faith goes a long way.

The next day I hired a local moving company and moved my belongings into my new home. They charged me $75, the exact amount of money that Angelo had thrown at me. Everything changed within those two weeks. In 1983, God Positioning Spirit welcomed me back with embracing love. It was a miracle to remind me "not to lose sight of common sense and discernment." Jojo and I quickly settled into our new home.

Transformation

Early one morning, I received a phone call that Mom had passed away. Jojo and I immediately drove to Ed's house to freshen up before the funeral. Mom's husband, Fernando, asked me to meet him at the funeral chapel parking lot. He said he was unable to deliver Mom's wig because the mortuary make-up artists were on strike and were blocking the entrance. When I drove up behind his pickup truck, I had a momentary shock when I saw Mom sitting in the passenger side. I realized instantly that it was her wig on a stand. I remembered the happier days when Mom sat next to Fernando. After I parked, he gave me her wig and makeup bag, and then drove away.

I went into the chapel with my mom's belongings and the dress that I had bought for her and handed them over to the woman attendant. She soon returned and led me into the viewing room where Mom lay in her coffin. She was wearing her wig and favorite dress. The lady reminded me that they were unable to apply her makeup because of the strike. She left the room. Music filtered into the room that sounded like angels softly singing, *Amazing Grace*. As soon as I opened Mom's makeup bag, I got a whiff of her fragrance and sensed her presence in the room. Tears welled up in my eyes when the first thing I noticed was her new favorite lipstick. It triggered a memory filled with sadness. As a little girl I often tried to hold onto Mom, to keep her at home, by hiding her favorite lipstick. I knew it was her finishing touch before she walked out the door and into the night.

I believe GPS aligned everything for me to experience this moment; to bring closure to those hurtful memories through my expression of love by applying Mom's finishing touch with her favorite lipstick, as if saying, "Okay, Mom, now you look beautiful. The door is open. Enter heaven's eternal light."

I whispered, "I love you, Mommy."

From a woman's perspective, I appreciated Mom's determination to achieve a better life even though the consequences had been too much to bear. Mom loved my little brothers. She was attentive to her new family, and at least I got to see her happy for a short while. I allowed the tears to flow as I remembered the day Mom had rejected me when I was 14 years old by shutting the door in my face. I thought how ironic that she experienced a similar rejection from her husband. From that point on, Mom had neglected her health and diabetes took its course, ultimately destroying her heart. I was thankful for our journey together. I was thankful she was my Mommy.

When Jojo graduated from high school, it became a festive time and served as a family reunion. Ed's arrival completed the celebration. Everyone had fun, especially while taking our first family pictures at a photography studio. Our family was finally and fully restored. Time had healed all the wounds from our tumultuous past. The rapturous, joyous festivities soon came to an end. Everyone departed, including Jojo, since she had decided to attend college in San Jose and live with her dad.

My house was empty, but I did not feel alone. I was filled with the warmth and joy of having my family together. I turned on my favorite *Jonathan Livingston Seagull* music and began cleaning the house, reflecting on and savoring the experience. I found Jojo's graduation gown draped over the armchair. I picked it up and breathed in her scent, recalling her laughter, remembering pivotal moments we shared, the fun she and I had getting her license, and her frantic voice saying, "Mom what about my prom dress?" It seemed like only yesterday when I was holding her in my arms as a baby. Now, here she was all grown up, ready to start the next chapter of her life.

As Neil Diamond's song, *"Be"* began to play, and as I dipped my feet in the pool, I watched the small ripples expand to the other side.

Then it hit me: my baby was gone—no more rushing and taking her to school, no more games with friends and no more last minute running around because she had forgotten or lost something.

I began to wonder what I was going to do with my life? The better question was: what was my identity? What was my purpose in life? I thought about each of my kids now living healthy, restored lives as God had promised me. Deep in thought, I attempted to figure out the next phase of my life. The words to the song, *Be,* quickened my heart. I felt God Positioning Spirit's loving presence speak to me through the lyrics:

"I was lost, but a painted sky spoke deep into my soul: Find him in a distance shore, by the wings of dreams I may know him. Be. Timeless theme one God will make for my day. You may know him."

My heart began to flutter and I was filled with love and joy. I began dancing and swaying, my hands extended up, loving God and His faithfulness. Tears flowed down my face in appreciation of Father God. The song, *"Dear Father,"* began to play, each lyric word speaking to me: *"We dream while we wait, who are we to need while we wait."* Every word touched my soul and left me with questions: *What are my dreams?* Every word touched my soul and left me with questions: *"Where do I go from here"*?

Carmen's last prophecy had been fulfilled: *Heal the children.* I heard her words, all those years ago, *"It's time for you to realize that God is calling you. You will receive confirmation when seven things happen. You have free will to choose."* Decision time was coming.

Soul Searching

I decided to sublet my house, hit the highway, and explore nature, trusting the journey to unfold as I went. Rudy, a life-coaching client of mine mentioned an interest in renting my house. He had a loaded Ram truck that had two gas tanks, CB radio and doublewide tires with a storage bin. We bartered first and last month's rent in exchange for the use of the truck. I packed my personals and other living essentials, placed my oversized teddy bear next to me, put on my cowboy hat, and headed straight for Highway 10.

Several miles into Arizona, in the middle of a pure, empty desert, I was captured by the winter full moon. It was beautiful and breathtaking. The truck's puttering sound caught my attention. I had forgotten to check the gas gauge. I needed to switch to the other gas tank. I left the motor on, got under the truck, and made the switch. Just like the gas switch, I made a mental switch not to be fazed or scared, thinking about snakes, spiders, and other creepy crawling creatures. It's amazing how quick we're able to switch thoughts instantly from fear to survival mode.

After hours of driving, I became sleepy. I stopped at the first motel I saw, paid for my room, and passed out. I was up at dawn and on the road with a cup of coffee. The CB radio chats between truck drivers were entertaining. I was in the fast lane, when I noticed a converted yellow school bus in the slow lane. As I passed it, I did a double take and my stomach flip-flopped. It was Jack! My body trembled with fear. I panicked. I was terrified that he'd seen me.

I immediately slowed down and swerved off the freeway into a truck stop. I ran into the bathroom and threw up everywhere. I was shaking uncontrollably and feeling faint. I sat on the commode, realizing that for nearly twenty years, fear and trauma had been stored in every cell of my body. Little by little, I released the trauma and began to feel freer. It was obvious that over the years I had stored toxic emotions relating to Jack. They were finally purged. I wondered how those memories had influenced many of my decisions in the past.

Still weak from the experience, I got back into the pickup truck. I was ready to go back home. What were the chances of seeing Jack and having those stored toxic emotions of him released? I was amazed. I concluded my road trip with a visit to New Mexico for a short stay and then returned home. It felt good to be home again, Rudy moved out into a smaller place. I lived in the house for almost a year, but was unable to keep up the payments, and eventually lost my beautiful ranch-style house. *"Truly a gift from God"*

A New Beginning

I finally overcame the fear of being alone, the single syndrome, and created a new identity of Entrepreneur Consultant, big words that indicated I needed to be resourceful and create income quick. I invested in self-help audio programs. Combined with my faith and determination I was able to create a personal blueprint with clear distinction what I needed to do different to support my goals. I rented an apartment in Costa Mesa and continued to build my spiritual-based, life-coaching business and workshops. Sometimes I was invited to facilitate adolescent group therapy my new life began to take form. First major step was when I accepted my new identity as a single woman, and spent my time reading history and personal development books. I was constantly learning. Even though I was helping people to help themselves, I still felt something was missing.

One morning I went out for a cup of tea at a quaint coffee shop. Sitting outside, I saw a man reading a newspaper. On the back page, were the bold words, *Transform Fear Into Power*. It struck a chord with me. I wondered, is that possible? It was as if GPS was speaking to me. Sipping on the tea, the fragrance reminded me of my special intimate times with GPS many years prior before I chose to re-route my life. From my purse, I took out a small journal and began to write about the other side of fear, how different my life looked from that perspective.

Later that evening, I decided to dress up, and treat myself to dinner at the Westin Hotel. It was a beautiful, southern California evening, and even though I wearing my high heels, I decided to walk. Entering the hotel, I heard the sounds of high-energy people coming from one of the meeting rooms. I followed it until I came across a large group of people standing in front of closed doors, eagerly waiting to enter the ballroom. As I got closer, I could hear loud, upbeat music. Suddenly, the doors opened and I was caught up in the wave of energetic people who drew me inside. I stood near the exit, not knowing what to expect. Everybody went to their seats but remained standing, still full of energy. My heart was pounding. I had never experienced anything like this before. It was so powerful, so empowering and so alive. My brain tried to make sense of it.

All of a sudden, a tall, young man appeared on stage, clapping his hands, keeping up with the beat of the loud music, along with everyone else in the room. He had an infectious laugh and a huge, radiant smile. He was exuberant, with a strong, spiritual presence. He started talking about things that resonated with me, things such as love, values, how one person can make a difference, passion for life, "the dream is possible", and much more.

He instructed the audience to close their eyes. I closed my eyes. Just then, Neil Diamond's *Prologue* came through the speakers at full volume, followed by *Father God* and closed with *Be*. Again, GPS aligned the moment: "Be still and know . . . I am loved." Immediately, my loneliness was replaced with peaceful assurance. My reasoning factor and spirituality united into a sense of *"Knowing" the Power of "Be"* to hear *The Still Small Voice"*

The music stopped. I noticed people taking off their shoes. The doors opened and the young man walked outdoors. Everybody followed him, including me. I ran to the bathroom, took off my nylons and high heels, and left them next to the trash bin. As I walked out the door, I found everyone standing on the other side of what appeared to be a hot bed of coals, celebrating. I approached the tall man. I felt his compassion and loving spirit, as if he looked right into my soul. He said, "Look up and walk." His words resonated deep within me. I had heard those very words before from GPS. I looked up, walked across glowing hot coals, and got to the other side, celebrating with the others. The tall, young man gave me a hug and a welcoming smile. Later that evening I learned his name was Tony Robbins, and the event I had walked into was his first Unlimited Power Weekend.

After that, I was hungry to learn more. I attended many other leadership training programs, like Dale Carnegie, Steven Covey and read numerous personal development books and continued with Bible Studies. I also continued to volunteer for several Tony Robbins events. He was offering a special event called "Date With Destiny" at his residence, known as "The Castle," in Del Mar, California. I was determined to attend, so I swallowed my pride and called Angelo, to ask for a loan.

He was happy to hear from me. I met him for coffee and talked about everything. I learned he had open-heart surgery, but was optimistic about his condition. We sat for hours talking like old friends, laughing and talking about our families. He asked how he could help me. I told him about my "Fire Walk" experience, what I had learned about turning fear into power, and what that meant for me. Like a paternal soul, he listened intently, concerned that I was caught up with some "quack," as he put it. I assured him that it was nothing like that. We said goodbye, knowing that both of us had moved on with our lives. I still loved him very much.

I remembered that at one of Tony Robbins' events, he spoke about relationships and that we should know what we desire. He said that before he met his wife, he described her on paper. That night I went home, played Neil Diamond's *Jonathan Livingston Seagull*, prayed for guidance, and wrote out a three-page description of my ideal husband. I desired from my heart and not from need, hoping that one day I would meet this God-appointed man and obtain a fulfilling and meaningful marriage.

Unexpectedly, I was given an extra scholarship for someone to attend the Unlimited Power Weekend in Long Beach, California. I called each of my kids to see if they wanted to attend. Regretfully, each one was unable to attend so I opted to stay home. No sooner had I called to take my name off the crew list, when my oldest son, Danny, who was now a firefighter and had his own family, called and said he wanted to attend. It was a miracle because he was the one child I least expected to go. I immediately called and put my name back on the crew list. I could not wait to see my son. When he arrived, the event had already begun and the ballroom was filled with hundreds of people.

There were times I lost sight of Danny. For one particular exercise, everyone was getting into groups. I, with many other volunteers, walked around the room. I could see my son engaged in a discussion within a group. A man in the group, who had buddied up with Danny, had his eyes closed, recalling an experience that had deeply affected his life. With a concerned look on his face, Danny signaled me to come over to help him. His buddy's story was becoming too intense. I went over to his group, approached the man and assured him that he was in a place of love and forgiveness. I asked him to slowly open his eyes. When he did, I could see the love and compassion in the heart of this man. Everyone surrounded him with love and hugged him.

After the event let out for the night, everyone went back to their hotels. Danny asked if I could pick him up later because he wanted to hang out with his new buddy, Rick. I stayed behind and helped clean up, and when I was finished, I went to meet Danny and Rick at the hotel. I found them at a bar with a group of people, talking. Danny introduced me to Rick. We said our goodbyes, and then left the hotel. As we waited for the valet to bring my car, I saw Rick driving by with a woman next to him.

I noticed his license plates plastic frame had a crack on the outer edge. The plate itself read, *"I'd rather be sailing."* I had a déjà vu moment". I remembered a dream I had of that same license plate with a cracked plastic frame and the plate reading, "I'd rather be sailing." Stunned, I kept this to myself. The next day, I returned to the event and said goodbye to Danny, who had to leave a day early.

Rick approached me and asked if I was coming back on the following day. I said yes. He asked me to join him for coffee after the event. He was an intriguing man and a great conversationalist. I had no interest in dating him or anyone else at that time because I was busy building my business and I was having an amazing journey in life.

Several weeks later, I received a bouquet of flowers at my office with an invitation to dinner from Rick. I drove to San Diego and met him at a beautiful coast-side restaurant. We talked about everything, from sailing and golf to traveling and life in general. At the end of dinner, I thanked him and told him that if he wanted another date with me, he would have to fill out a questionnaire. I wanted to see his values and know more about him. Just like an employer who interviews a potential candidate to see if the person is qualified for the position, we both reviewed and discussed my questionnaire. I wanted to see if he was dating material. He looked at it, as if to say,

"You've got to be kidding," but respectfully agreed like a gentleman. We made a date to meet later at the Marriott Hotel in San Diego.

The day came for our date. I arrived at the hotel and went up the escalator to the lounge area. I looked out the window that overlooked the piers and saw Rick stepping out of a docked sailboat. As he walked towards the hotel, I clearly heard God say, "He is your husband." I recalled the lyric to the song, Be: "I was lost but a painted sky spoke deep into my soul: Find him in a distance shore, by the wings of dreams I may know him." My knees quivered. I was not ready for this.

We exchanged our completed questionnaires. Without reading them, we just talked and enjoyed our dinner. After we finished, Rick walked me to my car. He gave me an auto card and a gas card. "Be safe," he said. "I look forward to seeing you again."

We continued to date. We went sailing, had fun, and developed a good friendship. After six months, he asked me to marry him. I told him I did not love him. My heart was still recovering from Angelo. He said he understood, and that he loved me enough to wait. He asked me to take a trip with him to Canada and I agreed. As soon as I got home, I became confused. It was unfair to Rick because I was still in love with Angelo. I called him that night and told him I could not accept his proposal. He would not take no for an answer. He said he was on his way to pick me up. I told him not to call me or pick me up, and I hung up. I grabbed a bottle of Nyquil and downed it so I could sleep.

In my drunken Nyquil stupor, I called Angelo. I poured out my heart to him. While I was talking, someone was knocking at my door. I opened it with the phone still in my hand. I gave it to Rick who was standing there. I went to my bedroom and continued crying. After a few minutes, Rick knocked on my door, gave me the phone, and said "Angelo wants to talk to you."

"Go with him," Angelo told me. "He's a good man and has the right intentions. You know I will always be here for you, my girl. Goodbye." I knew it was over.

Rick and I headed to Canada. I felt sad that Angelo had let me go, that I would never see him drive up and hear his foot-steps at my door, or the phone ring and hear his voice. I also knew that releasing Angelo was a must for me to move forward and be present with Rick. It was finally over.

The weather was beautiful. I was able to enjoy nature while Rick kept his business appointments. On our return to the States, I made it clear that he was to meet my son, Paul. I would set up luncheon date for the three of us at the pier. He had already met Danny so it was essential that he meet Paul and then my girls. It soon became obvious that they got along great and had much in common. We continued dating. Rick's idea of dating was sailing, golfing and eating at the finest restaurants.

One night, at our favorite French restaurant in Newport, I knew he was up to something. Our usual table near the fireplace was beautifully set with long candles. I felt this was soon to become a moment of decision. The sommelier arrived and poured champagne. A violinist began to play and slowly moved a little closer to our table. Rick then pulled out a beautiful ring box and opened it, gazing into my eyes. Without hesitation, I accepted his proposal as we both looked at the gorgeous engagement ring as he placed it on my finger. Rick held onto my hands and said, "I love you, Deanna. I know one day you will feel the same."

We decided on a long engagement and moved to Santa Barbara. Our home, across from the mission, was perfect. I could hear church bells ring on Sundays. My coaching clientele began to grow. I had wonderful friends. I seldom cooked dinner because Rick and I enjoyed eating out. When we had been together six months, we hired a wedding consultant and spent the next six months planning our wedding. I found the perfect white wedding dress with rhinestones and re-moveable train. My three girls were to be my bridesmaids. My granddaughters, Chandrea and Victoria, would also be in the wedding party. I enjoyed making their flower girl dresses. My grandson's role was to serve as an usher and seat the guests. There was never a moment for me to reflect on my life or how I had come to this point.

The day before my wedding I checked into the hotel. I spent the evening reading, meditating, and journaling about the blessings that had unfolded since I had allowed GPS to lead the way in my life. Beverly, my matron of honor, arrived and we spent the rest of the evening finishing the last minute details. Late into the evening, we fell asleep.

On the morning of my wedding, the sun pierced through the shutters and woke me up. At almost the same time, the phone in my room rang. It was Angelo. "Hi. How's my girl? Just called to congratulate you."

I assured him I was doing well, then after a brief pause, he asked, "Do you love him?" With tears welling in my eyes, I said "yes." Satisfied, he said a tender goodbye and hung up. Looking out the window at the Pacific Ocean, I thought about my spontaneous and pure response to his question. I loved Rick, my husband to be. I really loved him.

By nine o'clock, my room filled up with my girls, Rick's mom, and my wedding consultant, fussing around me to get everything perfect for our noon wedding. By eleven, I sent them all away so I could spend time alone in prayer. As I looked below at the preparations going on, I could see them setting up the final touch, which was the flowered arch we would stand under to say our vows. I could see my grandsons seating the guests. Strains of the violin and the harp filtered up to me. They were playing my favorite music, "Somewhere In Time." Beverly came in to help me put on my dress and the veil. We prayed together and then she left. I could see below that every chair was filled with our friends and relatives. My sister, Silvia, along with Robert, who had finally stopped using drugs, his lovely wife Anna, and Rick's mom were all seated in front. For a moment, I could imagine Mom being there. She would have loved it.

My consultant knocked on the door, reminding me that I was running late. Before leaving the room, I looked back, and said *thank you*, as if speaking to GPS, knowing at that moment I was the total sum of my past. It filled me with joy. I looked below where my two sons dressed in tuxedos were ready to walk me to the altar.

My ideal husband stood before me, waiting to receive his bride-to-be. He was everything I had written on my list, all except one thing. I had written that I wanted a brown-skinned man. Instead, God gave me a wonderful, white, Scots Irishman with the last name of Brown. God surely has a sense of humor. Right after we exchanged our wedding vows and sealed our marriage, the bagpipers, dressed in Scottish attire, surprised us by playing, "Amazing Grace." Again, I sensed Mom, and thanked God.

I found married life very fulfilling. Rick and I had a whirlwind, lovely life filled with international travel. Most of my kids were married, except Paul. Jojo became engaged to John, every mother's dream son-in-law. We enjoyed every moment planning her wedding. When her day arrived, she had a spectacular church wedding and reception. All her brothers and sisters were in the wedding party. Rick's daughter Megan was also there. Ed, Rick and I had a wonderful time. It was lovely to see Jojo dance with her dad. Then as mother of the bride, it was my turn to dance with Ed. There are no words to describe the blessing of that moment, with our children and family watching as we danced to a lovely Mexican ballad. We were all together - As God promised our "*Restored Family*"

As the years passed, Rick and I moved to Sausalito above the Alta Mira Hotel on top of the hill. I began doing workshops again, building my coaching clientele. I thought I had finally reached the desired destination of my heart, and yet, there was an unfulfilled feeling. I sensed GPS tug at my heart: *Help my children.*

Tender Closure

Working late one night in my office, I received a call from Angelo's wife to let me know he had passed on. He never really recovered from the major heart surgery a few years earlier, and had somewhat given up on life. She shared that at the exact moment when he died at the hospital, his dog rolled over and died at home. I remembered when he had bought his four-week-old puppy. I thanked her and said good-bye, closing our common bond to a man we both loved, accepting our fate to let him go.

"Come to the edge," He said.
They said, "We are afraid."
"Come to the edge," He said

"They came. He pushed them . . . And they flew"

- Guillaume Apollinaire

Chapter Nine: Destiny

Repositioned for Purpose

Tony Robbins had another Unlimited Power Weekend event. This time it was in Burlingame, California. I had not volunteered for a few years because Rick and I traveled frequently on business. I felt the need to attend the event. Rick preferred that I didn't go because his daughter was coming out for a visit. I respected his request, but I felt restless. At the last minute, I sensed an urgent need to volunteer. This was unusual for me. Even though I was looking forward to spending time with Megan, I knew intuitively I had to go to this event. Rick understood and supported my decision.

Over a thousand people were lined up for registration. It was hectic but great to be there, helping to set up, meeting friends, and getting people registered. While at the registration tables, I noticed three yellow school busses from San Jose Eastside Unified High School District in front of the hotel. One by one, teenagers were lined up, preparing to enter the hotel. I immediately connected with them. It was amazing that this youth group came to learn life skills.

I heard a commotion in the corner of the hotel foyer. Some of the kids did not want to enter the event. They were escorted to another meeting room. I followed to see what was going on. The teenagers sat on the floor with their physiology closed off, as if to say, "leave me alone." I asked the coordinator if I could talk to them. She signaled me, without any words as if to say, "they are all yours." I began to talk to them, and for some reason we connected. I felt like the Pied Piper. They got up and followed me into the main ballroom.

On the last day of the event, I was busy and didn't see the teenagers. Suddenly I felt nauseous. I hurried to the bathroom, but there was a long line. I dashed out of the hotel ready to throw up. I saw the teens at a distance, gathered on the lawn, eating lunch with their chaperones. As soon as they saw me, they called my name and waved me over. Immediately the nausea vanished. They were eating hamburgers, which was not part of Tony Robbins' health program.

I went over and sat down with them. A girl handed me a hamburger. I was a vegan at the time, but I hesitantly took a bite. Just then, Tony came out and caught me biting into a hamburger instead of drinking green juice. The teenagers laughed. We all laughed, including Tony. It was funny. Tony talked to the group, and afterwards hugged them, said goodbye, and returned to the event.

It was obvious GPS had set me up again. If I had not felt nauseous, I would not have gone outside, and I would not have had the chance to hang out with embracing high school students before they left for their long trip back to San Jose. As they were boarding, I noticed the two gentlemen who had arranged for the kids to attend the event. I asked them, "What happens now?" One of them responded, "What do you mean?" I asked, "What's the follow-up?" He said there would be one last meeting at the school. I asked if I could attend and he said yes. As the busses began to depart, the teens pulled the windows down, yelling at me, "Hope to see you soon!"

God's Purpose Emerges

Two weeks later, I visited the school where most of the teens attended to discuss their experience. The two gentlemen, Mike and Joe, and some of the teachers and counselors were there. They asked the students what they had learned from the event. The teens openly shared their experiences and wrote them down. As they were writing, Joe and Mike excused themselves. I walked out with them and asked, "Is that it?"

They said, "Yes, that's it." My heart was heavy for these amazing kids who were labeled as "at risk" students. I was determined to change that. I felt I was handed an opportunity but did not know what it was at that time. I got back to the auditorium just as the students were walking out. They handed me their writing assignments.

That night, after arriving home, I read what they wrote. Tears streamed down my face. I knew the direction of my life had changed. The following week, I returned to each school and stood outside in the quad in hopes of seeing the students again—nothing the first week. I went three days a week, but for several weeks, none of the students came to the quad to meet with me. One day, a huge storm hit the Bay Area. I arrived at one of the schools. I stood and waited in the quad and again no students. The wind was so bad my umbrella turned inside out and I got drenched. I returned home, feeling frustrated. I said to my husband, "I don't think God was telling me to go to those schools." Rick responded, "Are you giving up?" I stomped out, grumbling to myself.

The following Monday afternoon, I returned to one of the schools. A school counselor came out from the administration office, walked towards me, and gave me a key. At that moment, I felt something. It was like an electric current flowing through me. She said, "They're waiting for you in Room 17." I walked into the classroom and greeted by a handful of students, only two of whom I recognized from the Tony Robbins event. I asked those two their first names and how things had changed since the event. They indicated their home life was better and that they were more focused on school. One of the girls brought her cousin to meet me. He had confided in her that he was contemplating suicide because he was having problems at home and hanging out on the streets. She pointed to him. He said, "She brought me here because this is the place where we can trust and talk to you." Another boy stood up and said, "We've been keeping an eye on you."

An hour passed and it was time for the students to leave. The boy that was going to commit suicide gave me a hug and said, "Thank you for listening, I feel better. See you next week." As I returned the key to the school counselor, who was standing outside, I informed her of the boy who was contemplating suicide, and asked her to follow up with him. I told her I would return the following week. My heart felt so much pain. If I had given up, what would have happened to that teenaged boy?

I returned home that night and told Rick, GPS inspired me to develop a curriculum, focused on the life lessons I had learned, combined with leadership skills specifically for this targeted group of kids labeled "at risk." Within ten days, by the Grace of God, the material and program were birthed.

The students eventually named their program, "Self Mastery CLUB," which stood for **C**ommitment, **L**eadership, **U**nity, and **B**elief. Gradually, more kids filled the after-school classroom program in various schools. Many of these kids had dropped out of high school. Many were gang-affiliated, young people who felt displaced, searching for meaning in their lives, from 14 to 18 years old. Many, who are now in their thirties, are still involved as alumni advisers and continue to contribute within their communities.

The Dream is Possible

One early morning, feeling under the weather and preoccupied with writing SMC class lessons for the week, the phone rang and I impatiently answered, "Yeah?" Then I heard, "Deanna?" I immediate recognized that unique voice: it was Tony Robbins! I was so embarrassed by how I had answered the phone.

Tony laughed, "Do you know who this is?" I also laughed, thinking, *of all the times to answer the phone the way I did!* He said, "This is Tony Robbins. I have you on speaker as a witness to this conversation. Deanna, I would like to invite you to be on the Board of Directors of the Anthony Robbins Foundation." The invitation was like God Positioning Spirit opening the door to help God's children: the hurting, forgotten souls, and to support Tony to fulfill his heartfelt vision to create global change and make a difference.

The trials we go through in life don't cease. They become part of our growth, refining us through the passage of life.

It's in our DNA (Divine Nature Access) to help others. It's through uncertainty, trials and error, that God reveals His love in a willing, open heart, to give and receive a miracle.

Before meeting my husband, Rick, my focus was on personal development. Rick was a successful businessman whose character was developed from mid-western, family values. He was a Texas A&M cadet, used to discipline and a corporate structure; all of which were completely opposite of me. I respected him and every value he embodied. We complimented each other by contrast. During our dating season, we became close friends and confidantes.

On our second date, we shared our values, beliefs, and heart-desires. Before our engagement, we agreed to place God first and build our relationship on trust, respect and contribution. The day we married, we honored a covenant of three: God, Rick and Deanna.

Life is like an oyster: when a grain of sand is placed inside, it irritates the oyster but the end-result is a beautiful pearl. Pain is like a grain of sand that repositions our life for purpose so that we may achieve peace and create positive differences as beautiful as a pearl. The pearl in itself has value, and it's up to us how we're going to display that value. All of my experiences became essential in positioning my life for purpose. I draw upon them daily to coach people to identify their spiritual, physical, and emotional significance. The outer world reflects man's heart. To make the Earth a better place for future generations, we must take responsibility for our own life, for our emotional and spiritual well-being.

In Summary

The highest lessons on trust are taught in the darkest of times. It's within those pivotal, painful moments of despair that purpose is revealed. The journey unfolds, driven by passion to make the crooked way straight. Pain comes in many forms, but there is one certainty: God created everything with intention, and His back-up plan is to fill and replenish with love and purpose. We don't have to travel alone.

GPS, "God Positioning (Holy) Spirit," is a master plan blueprint that is engraved on our souls. He will always meet us half way. Be still. Look within and know He has always been just a desire away.

God knew me way before I knew Him. The Holy Spirit comes not to give extraordinary signs, but to give new life to a broken heart and to give light to show us ourselves. It is not the size of our world that God sees, but the extent to which love fills our heart.

When I thought my life was a waste, God had the blueprint of my life and used unbearable pain to position me for purpose. Try this exercise to identify your life lessons and to create a visual blueprint. First, identify each painful experience. Second, describe what you learned from each one. It's your life. You might as well benefit from your pain, and transform those experiences so that they work for you. Third, become aware of how your past schooling in life defined your character, and realize that now you have the power to transform those experiences, to reposition your life for purpose, and to making a difference.

- Not having parents to guide me and instill their beliefs in me when I was young, I learned early to view life from different perspectives, to be inquisitive, and to follow my instincts.

- I learned early that life can be cruel, but I didn't need to stay stuck on stupid. If life hurts, allow your emotions to redirect your decisions that will change the direction in your life.

- Living with dysfunctional people and becoming one myself, I realized that life is a matter of choice. Look at your surroundings. Ask yourself how your choices reflect you and what you must do differently to redirect your life. Every time you notice a positive quality in another person, your hearts-desire is reflecting you to yourself.

- Our minds will recall experiences from which we need to learn. If you continue to attract the same people and situations creating the same pain, identify it, learn from it, and ask yourself the question: What must I do differently? Then change your approach! Eventually those people will leave and the situation will change.

- Since I was raised surrounded by gang-affiliated, drug and alcohol-addicted souls, they became my greatest source for lessons learned. My past experiences (painful as they were) gave me the tools to teach and have the compassion to be consistent and keep my commitment to teach "at risk," gang-affiliated youth. As a result, they touched and redirected my life and fulfilled my life purpose.

- Having been arrested and jailed twice, once for DUI and once for insufficient funds, I saw the unthinkable in the short time I was locked up. Even though those experiences were over 30 years ago, I draw upon them. They opened my heart and mind to understand women who have done dumb things in their lives, many for the sake of love. I know how one can feel trapped by it, especially seeing how decisions play out in children's lives. For many years, I taught empowering life skills at several prisons in Atlanta, Georgia, Houston and California. The message was always the same, "freedom resides within our heart and mind." To be honest, I see more imprisoned souls on the outside than in prison. The mind does not know on which side of the wall you live. My schooling in the world of hard knocks taught me so much. My first job after leaving my nursing career, was working with transitioning San Quentin ex-felons. They became my teachers. I saw so many wounded souls; hurting little boys trapped in a bad man's world. Taking all these situations into consideration—on the outside as well as on the inside of prison walls—there is freedom in Christ.

- When my son was sentenced to 25 years in prison, at that pivotal moment I knew as a mom, there were only two things I could do. First, keep my son in constant prayer, and second, not enable him to depend on me or anyone else. When the day of his release finally arrived, at the first sight of my son, I held my baby boy in my arms. Crying, I gave thanks to God that there was not one mark (tattoo) on my son's skin, which signified my answered prayer—God had protected my son. One of the first things Frank said to me when he got out was, "Mom, thanks for your tough love, I knew you had my back if I needed help within reason. That helped me stay focused and, most importantly, thanks for your prayers. I was a free man in prison."

- The greatest hardship that bruised my soul deeply was to be labeled mentally ill; and yet, that became my greatest awakening. To this day my heart feels for the lost, forgotten souls in mental institutions, many who are simply abandoned, left to slowly deteriorate, overshadowed in their mind and lost in darkness.

All the above examples and my own appointed downfalls and numerous obstacles, even at my worst when I was living in pure hell, were essential elements in that "God repositioned all my pain for purpose."

I have learned my greatest life lessons through trials. Regeneration of the soul is described as a new birth; the Holy Spirit like a mother gives birth to us, positioning us to fulfill our purpose on earth and prepare us for Heaven. It's sad how many die inside, feeling unloved, abandoned, only because we forgot to realize who we are and that the very thing we seek is seeking us—to make us whole. It is innate, within us, the driving force, searching for an open heart to fulfill its own desire through and for us.

In searching for myself externally, I never knew pure love existed, but all along GPS resided within me. Many say to me, "Come on, Deanna, do you really believe in God?" I emphatically answer, "Yes!" He heard my cry in the wilderness, as a dying soul. His loving touch restored my life. In searching for myself externally, I never knew pure love existed, but all along GPS resided within me.

As Rick Warren states in his book, *The Purpose-Driven Life*, it's not about you. Life has a greater purpose. How profound. We are made for a reason. How would you define your life, your purpose? What is driving you? Are you still calling "OnStar," instead of GPS?

When you feel a void, desperately seeking love and happiness, feel restless, or hit a dead-end or roadblock; your spirit is yearning for God, a one-on-one, direct spirit connection. Be still, see, feel, and know you have purpose. Stand up and dance to the beat of your heart and allow love to embrace you. When I embraced myself, welcomed and determined a move forward, it became the turning point in life.

Awakening to take responsibility, while having fun in the process of discovery, became the vehicle that allowed me to obtain my high school diploma, a nursing education, and my teaching credentials. GPS inspired me to create the Self Mastery Youth Leadership Curriculum-based program that has helped thousands of "at risk" youths gain hope and direction in their lives.

I realized life was never about me, but about what I could do differently to create change and instill empowering passion and validity in others. The point is that nothing is impossible, even for those who have lost hope and struggle on a daily basis.

Right now, look around you. Everything has significance. They are reminders of a call for action. If a girl like me, who grew up in poverty, was given away by her mother at 14, had seven children by the age of 23, seldom attended elementary school, and only had a seventh grade education could achieve her dreams, then there is hope for you, too. If you were fortunate and raised to have everything you wanted, that feeling of emptiness inside you is perhaps reminding you to volunteer and to be a gift to others.

Sometimes when life throws a curve ball and knocks us down, initially we ask, "why," but perhaps a better question is "who must I become and what must I do differently in the process of discovery to reposition my life in a different direction?" Metaphorically, when we're driving in a car and we hit a roadblock or get lost, GPS (God Positioning Spirit) becomes the source that provides assurance and guides us to our destination.

"The main ingredient for success: Love who you see in the mirror!"

The most amazing experience about life is the souls God positions for us to meet at every crossroad. Angels in work clothes are sent as reminders that we can make it the rest of the way.

"We are not human beings having a spiritual experience; we are spirit beings having a human experience." - **Pierre Teilhard de Chardin**

Process of Discovery

To heal our soul, we must take responsibility and live by the standard we desire from others. We are the landlords of our minds; we must become selective and allow only thoughts that add value to our lives and evict those that cause us problems. We don't think twice about evicting squatters who invade our physical property; we remember to change the filter of our car on a regular basis because if we don't, the consequence is costly. And we also remember to delete trash on our computer hard-drive to keep it safe. We must take responsibility to weed out the garden of our mind daily.

"Happiness is our Birthright"

My personal set-up was expecting from my parents what they did not demonstrate in their own lives. How could I expect love from them if they didn't know how to express it? Impressions can change. You are never too young or old to envision and have a better life.

- Ask yourself: Do I believe with enough intensity to achieve desired results or do I feel something is keeping me in the dark, causing reoccurring pain?

Exercise

- Step outside of the painful memory, and see what you have taken in as truth, that which is keeping you in the dark. "Turn on" the internal light switch of your mind. Ask yourself: How do you and your loved ones benefit from that pain filled memory yearning to be revealed, forgiven and transformed to help others restore their soul.

Learned Lesson Summary

- You cannot change people; in fact, when you expect more from others, you will subject yourself to disappointments.

- Feeling powerless minimizes your chances of making healthy life choices. It increases your vulnerability to make spontaneous decisions for immediate gratification, which usually has long-term consequences.

- Identify undesirable effects and trace back to its cause. Then change your approach to the situation.

- Trials in your life serve to refine your character and open your heart's desire, instills compassion, which is needed to fulfill your destiny so you will become a pioneer for change helping others in the targeted areas that caused the most pain in your life.

Stop Comparing Yourself: Embrace your spirit. God predestined and created you with intention. Follow the same intention and live with defining purpose. You are a unique expression of God. Invest in your dream with determination to fulfill your destiny. You are a work in progress. Don't stop moving forward because someone left you. Anyone who leaves you did not love you enough to share life's obstacle course with you.

It's good not to live in ignorance, but to have clear distinction what you personally feel called to accept as your truth. Ask yourself how your life reflects your spiritual beliefs? Do you feel a void in your heart? Imagine yourself walking with Christ Jesus or Buddha what would you want to ask them? Then search out for answers and if you still come void, ask God Positioning Holy Spirit for insight and guidance. Over 30 years ago when I learned about Jesus, the son of God who was a man that lived here on earth, his message transformed and saved my life. I have enjoyed learning about comparative religion studies in, eastern philosophy and holistic teachings. Traveling extensively I learned to embrace other people religious practices as I would like others to embrace mine; equally with love as we learn we're all one big family. Call out, "God help me." Admit you need help. He knows your heart-filled emotional pain. Where others have turned away God desires to be your personal navigator moving forward to fulfill your destiny.

God has given us his Spirit as proof that we live in him and him in us.
— 1John 4:13

Final Thoughts From the Author

You don't have go through life alone. I hope you keep in touch with me and perhaps share how reading this book has impacted your life. I will personally read and answer your emails. I look forward to meeting with you at one of my seminars.

I pray that somehow my stories will give you insight that your life counts. God created you with gifts, which are waiting for you to unveil, your personalized magnificent tapestry to humanity. Sometimes we don't always see how our gifts link us together in fulfilling our destiny because when life feels unfair, it blindsides us from seeing the benefit and value of how significant we are. Every tool and resource needed to adapt to the process of transforming your life is within reach. Every resource is fulfilled before our time to ensure we don't take the journey alone.

From Despair to Destiny

One day I was inspired to spend quality time with each of my children. The goal was to acknowledge them for being amazing souls, thanking them for their love, and to ask forgiveness for the hardships and the pain they endured growing up. And then, with an open heart, I just listened!

Memorable Moment:

One day, a few years before writing this book, I went to visit my oldest son, Danny, to just "hang" for a few days. We took a drive for coffee, talking about life and family. We parked outside the house. I felt inspired to apologize for the hardship he experienced growing up: "I am sorry, my son."

He turned his face, looking out of his pickup truck window. I could see a tear roll down his face and in his loving, nurturing way, he said, "Mom, you know we all turned out pretty good. We're a close, loving family." He laughed, gave me a hug and said, "All is good mom, we pulled through," adding that I should write my life story. "Maybe it could help someone struggling like we did, and will give them hope that those times will pass, and they can stay together like we did. Our family is tight, Mom."

Tribute to My Children

Jojo: Insightful discerning spirit and rational perspective adds value to what presents itself.

Megan: A Petite stature resides an awakened soul, driven to live on purpose and save lives

Karyn: Spiritually guided nurturing heart, driven by purpose to help hurting forgotten souls

Hope: Sense of humor, love and determination to pick up slack when and where needed

Frank: Steadfast commitment to add value to others, while learning to walk free again

Paul: Integrity based creative loving soul where associates and family turn to for guidance.

Sandi: Loving hugs, laughter and open door home policy is like "chicken soup for the soul"

Danny: loving giant with a warriors heart, an Eagles perspective with readiness to help others

Thank you for sharing the journey forward
Love Mom

I took the long hard road and got lost in the wilderness. We're not spared from difficult journeys, but it makes a huge difference knowing that we have options available for the asking: Lifetime warranty insurance, pre-paid coverage, all-inclusive, GPS. "Your personal navigator upon request."

Enjoy the journey and have fun in the process of discovery.

Blessings to you,
Deanna Brown

CONTACT: DEANNA BROWN

"Life is a spiritual assignment with responsibility to discover our Divine purpose"

One - One Strategic Personalized Coaching:

I believe God instilled every soul with innate gifts essential to add value to mankind. Through a personalized process of discovery you will learn essential life changing tools and skills that will transform and reposition your life for purpose.

www.deannabrown.com   Life Coach

Self-Mastery Youth Leadership SMYL

Deanna offers certification training to teach the Self Mastery Youth Leadership Program that is specifically developed for the At Risk youth population. This program is ideal for after school programs, home studies, and juvenile correctional and treatment centers.

www.selfmasteryinstitute.com

Is Your Organization Planning Retreats?

Process of Discovery Transformational Workshops are specifically designed for those ready to receive life changing insight, tools and skills that will reposition their life for purpose.

www.deannabrown.com

Monthly Facilitated Mentoring Forum

If you like the idea of informal group connections on specific topics the forum is for you. It provides the value and benefit from Deanna's intuitive coaching perspective combined with the collective insights from like- minded peers.

Speaking Engagements:
E-mail her direct: deanna@deannabrown.com

Deanna Brown has personally implemented life changing results through process of discovery workshops specifically designed for youth and women within the correctional system and transitional residential programs. For more information about these workshops, email **deanna@deannabrown.com**.

A FREE sample of Deanna Brown's ***Process of Discovery Workbook*** is available on her website at **www.DeannaBrown.com**.

Share your reading experience:
E-mail deanna direct: deanna@deannabrown.com

5211666R00084

Made in the USA
San Bernardino, CA
28 October 2013